9108
P9-DFB-658

NO LONGER THE PROPERTY OF
BALDWIN PUBLIC LIBRARY

INSECTLOPEDIA

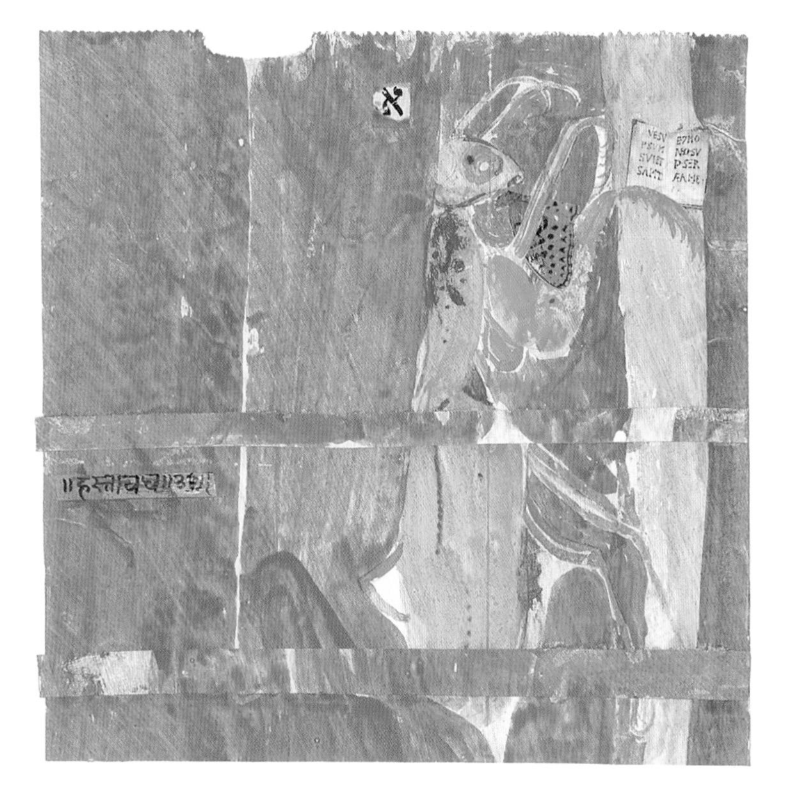

POEMS AND PAINTINGS BY

DOUGLAS FLORIAN

VOYAGER BOOKS • HARCOURT, INC.

SAN DIEGO • NEW YORK • LONDON

www.harcourt.com

First Voyager Books edition 2002
Voyager Books is a trademark of Harcourt, Inc., registered in
the United States of America and/or other jurisdictions.

The Library of Congress has cataloged the hardcover edition as follows:
Florian, Douglas.
Insectlopedia: poems and paintings/by Douglas Florian.
p. cm.
Summary: Presents twenty-one short poems about such insects as
the inchworm, termite, cricket, and mayfly.
1. Insects—Juvenile poetry. 2. Children's poetry, American.
3. Insects in art—Juvenile literature.
[1. Insects—Poetry. 2. American poetry.] I. Title.
PS3556.L589I57 1998
811'.54—dc20 96-23029
ISBN 0-15-201306-7
ISBN 0-15-216335-2 pb

G H

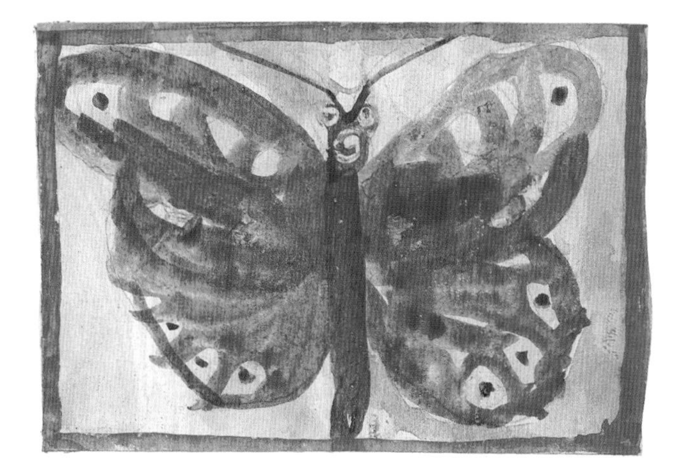

This book is for

Zoe and Rose Birnbaum
Ore, Liane, and Ilil Carmi
Zoe and Victoria Goldenberg
Calla Henkel
Eamon Johnston
Natanel, Elinore, and Dorine Lallouche
Chaya, Beila, and Sarah Leboeuf
Moshe and Maya Madjar
Molly McTague
Dafna, Adam, and Chaya Mushka Mendelson
Stephanie, Ian, Rebecca, and Vaughn Pfeffer
Ariel and Michael Podwal
Emily and Michael Theodore

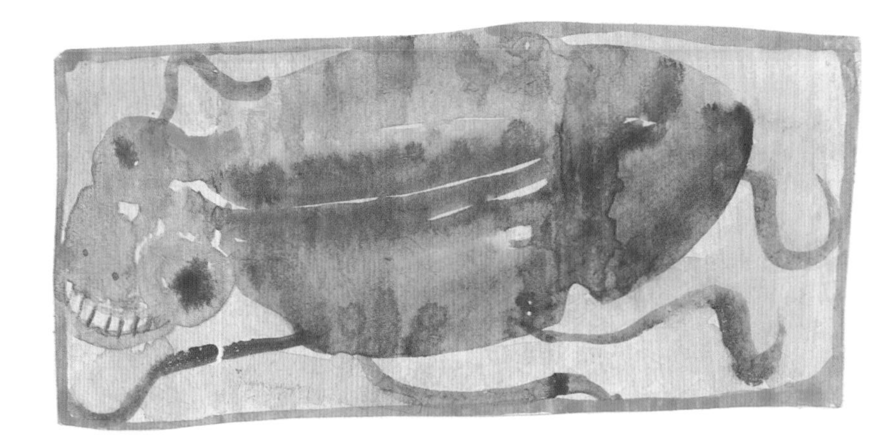

Contents

The Caterpillar

She eats eight leaves at least
To fill her,
Which **leaves** her like a
Fatterpillar,
Then rents a room inside
A pupa,
And checks out: Madame Butterfly—
How super!

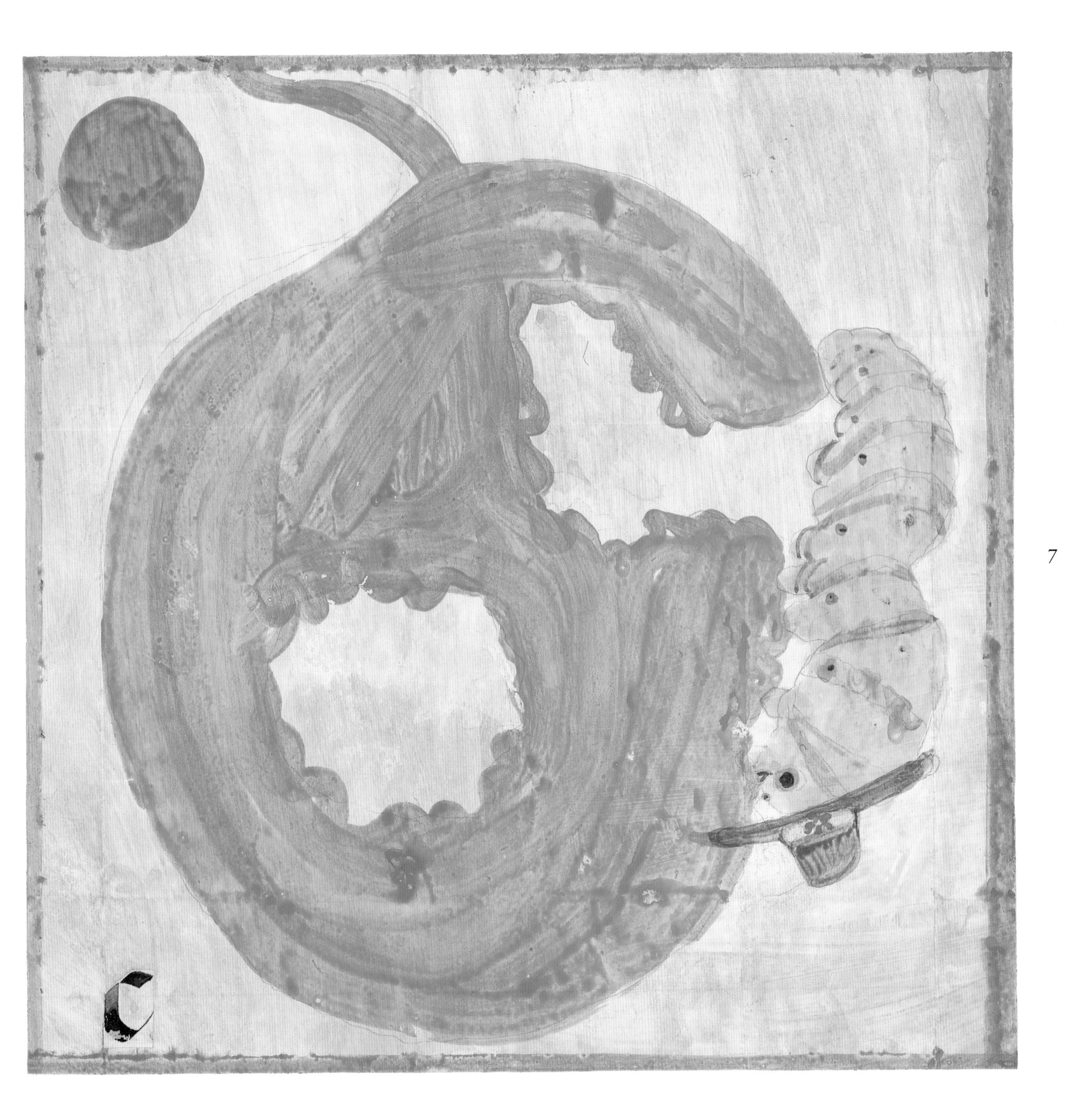
C

The Dragonfly

I am the dragon,
The **demon** of skies.
Behold my bold
Enormous eyes.
I sweep
        I swoop
                I terrorize.
For lunch I munch
On flies and bees.
Mosquitoes with
My feet I seize.
I am the dragon:
Down on your knees!

The Daddy Longlegs

O Daddy
Daddy O
How'd you get
Those legs to grow
So very long
And lean in size?
From spiderobic
Exercise?
Did you drink milk?
Or chew on cheese?
And by the way,
Where are your knees?
O Daddy
Daddy O
How'd you get
Those legs to grow?

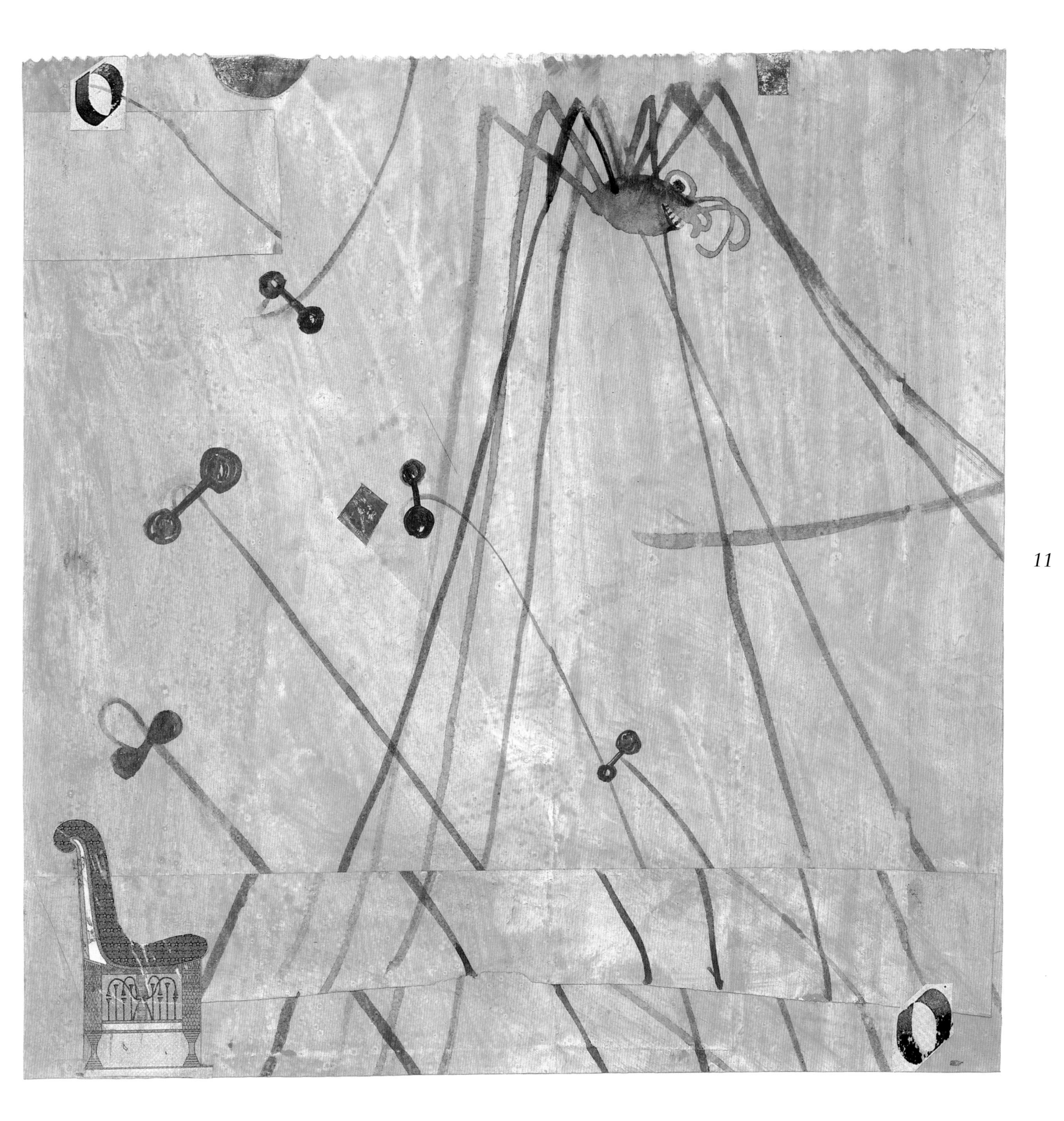

The Army Ants

Left
Right
Left
Right
We're army ants.
We swarm.
We fight.
We have no home.
We roam.
We race.
You're lucky if
We miss your place.

The Inchworm

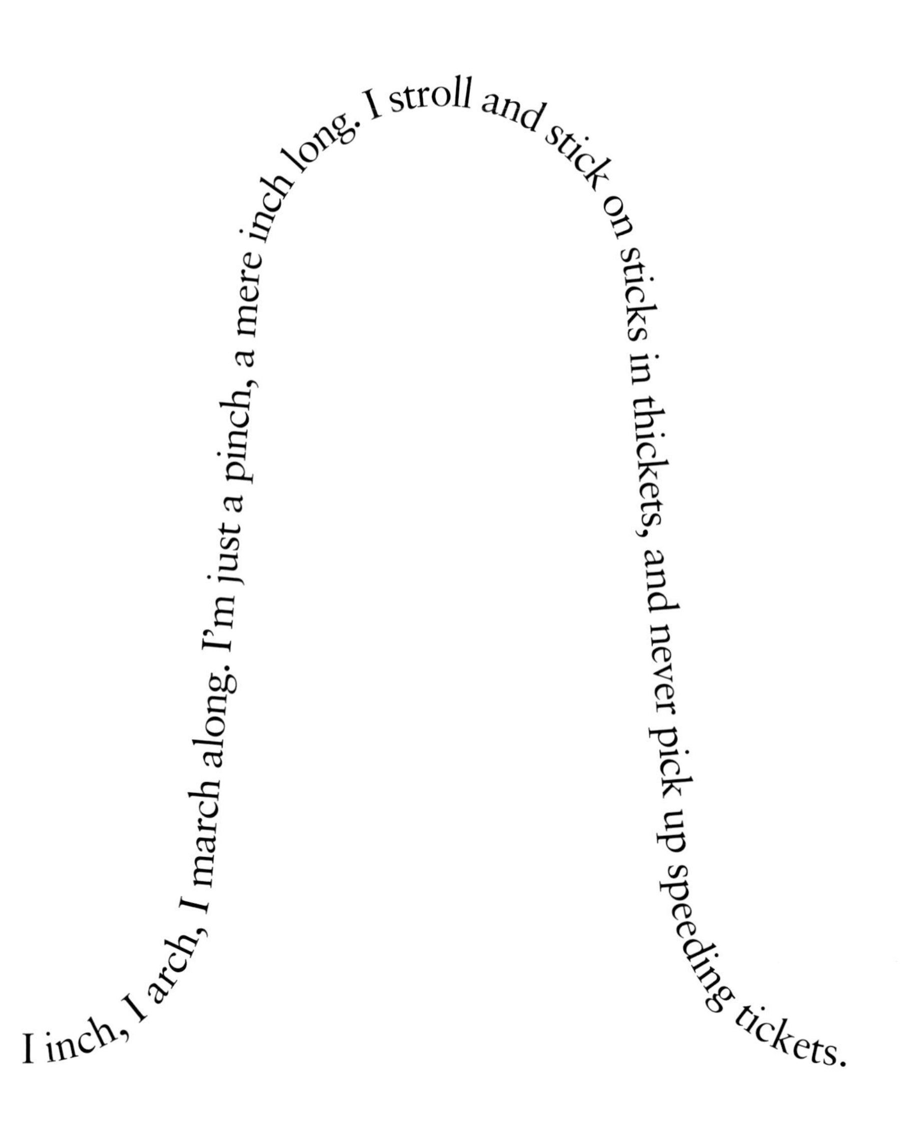
I inch, I arch, I march along. I'm just a pinch, a mere inch long. I stroll and stick on sticks in thickets, and never pick up speeding tickets.

R R
55
Sh

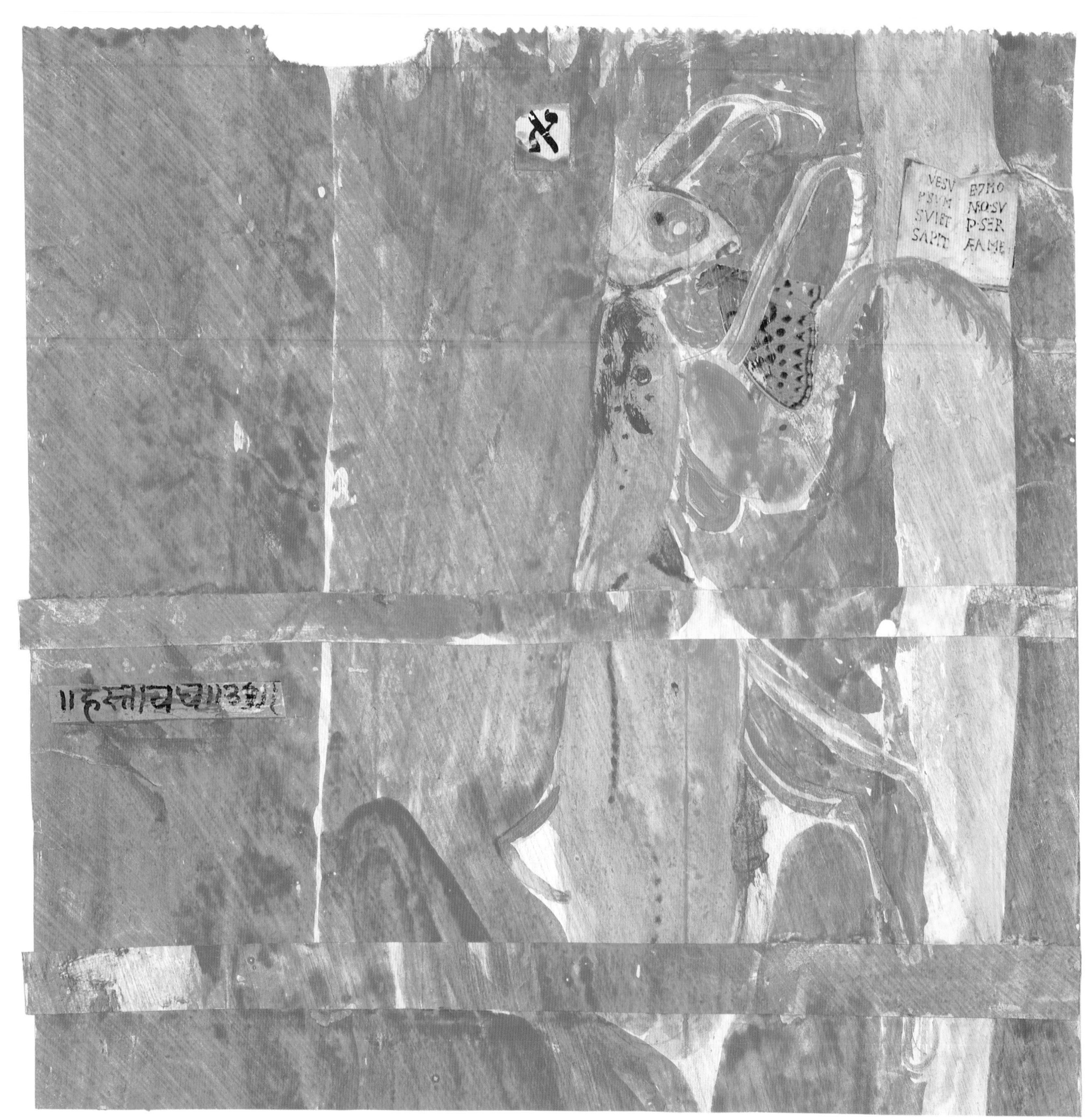

16

The Praying Mantis

Upon a twig
I sit and pray
For something big
To wend my way:
A caterpillar,
Moth,
Or bee—
I swallow them
Religiously.

The Black Widow Spider

I am a widow—
I always wear black,
From my eight dainty legs
To my shiny round back.
Do not disturb me.
My fangs carry venom.
I am a widow—
I don't wear blue denim.

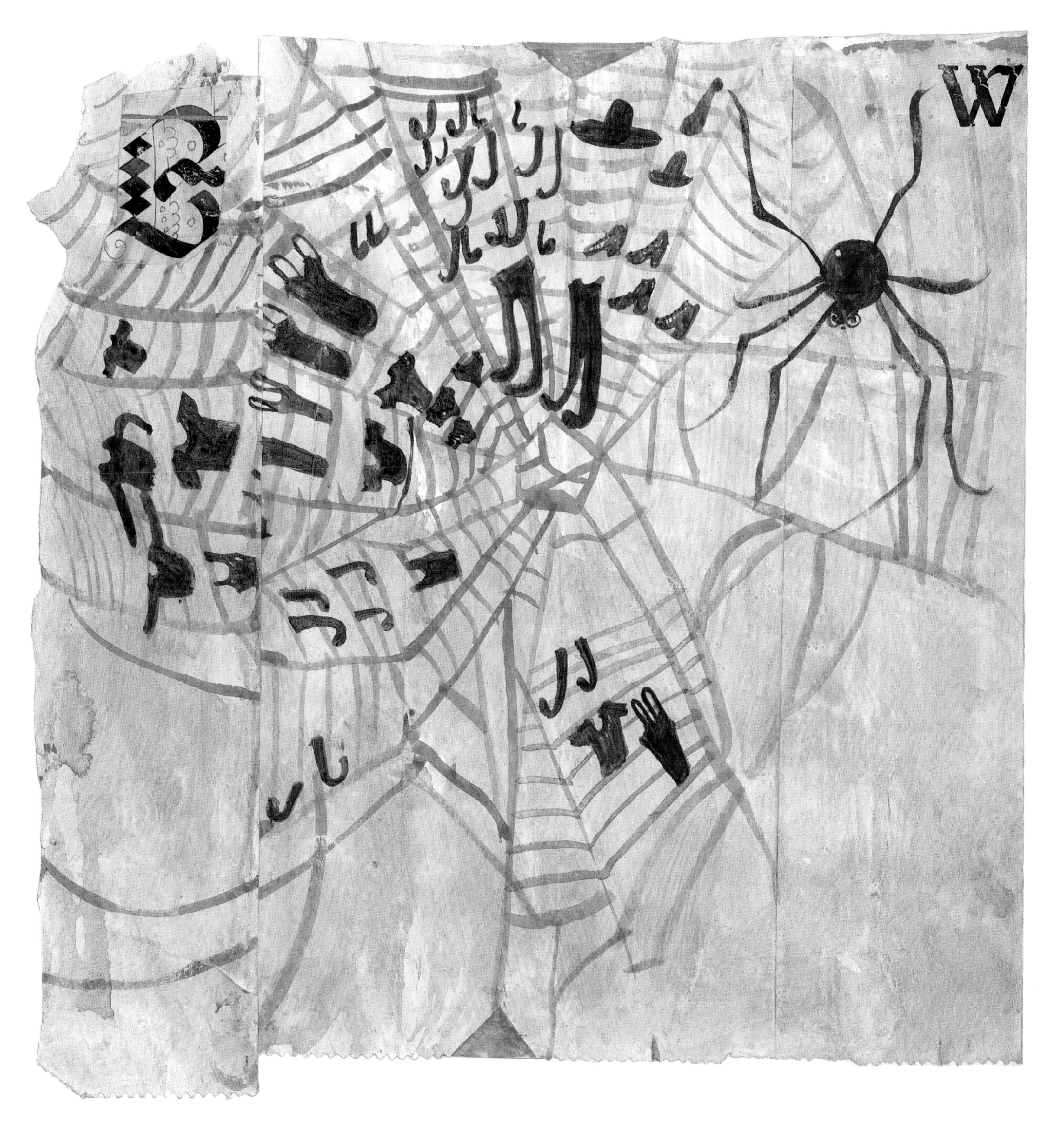
W

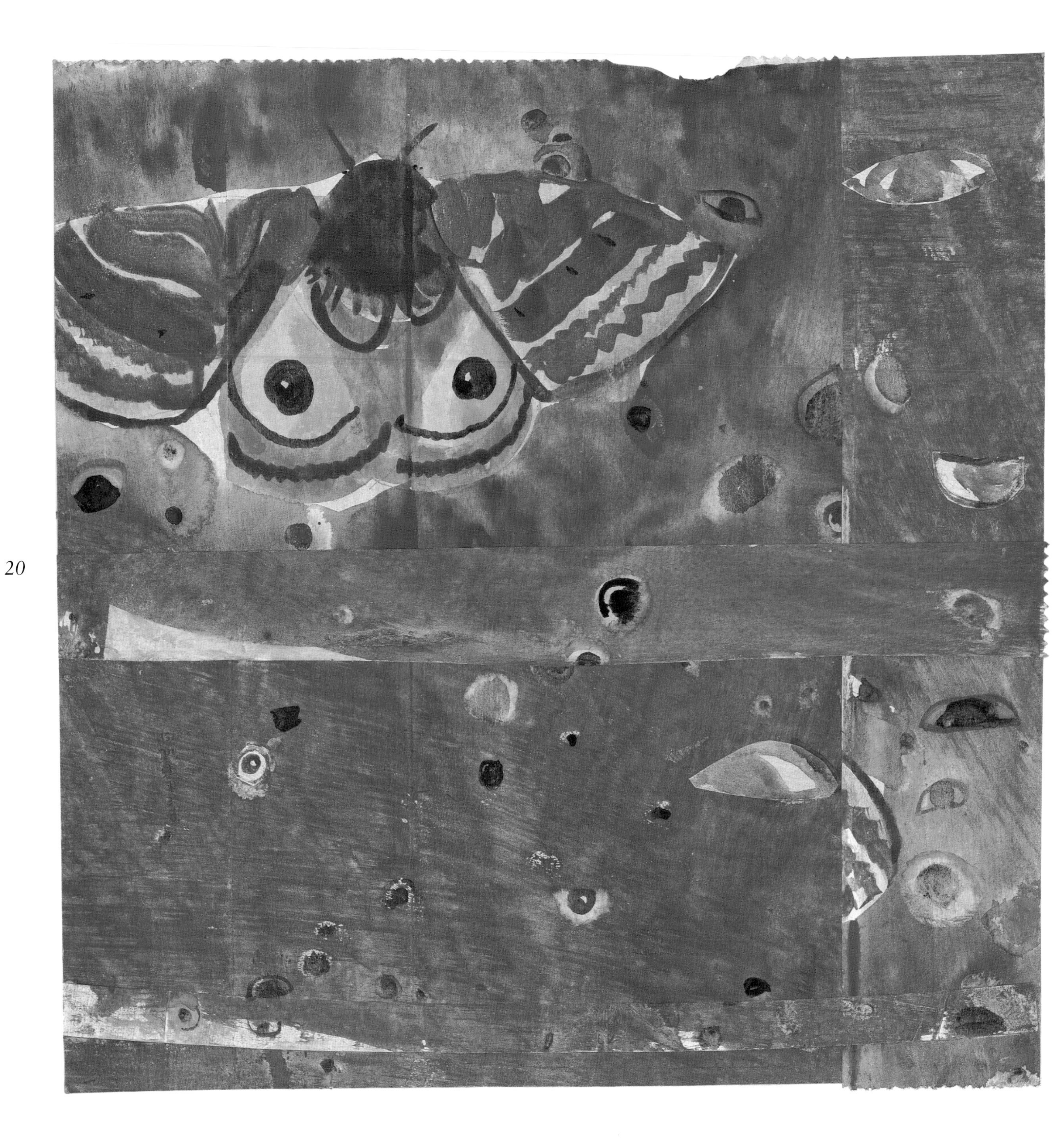

The Io Moth

The io moth
Has mam-moth eyes
That are not real—
They're a disguise
To ward off birds
And other creatures,
Like garter snakes
And science teachers.

The Whirligig Beetles

We
whirl,
we
twirl,
we
skate,
we
glide.
Upon
a
pond
or
lake
we
.ride
We
swim
in
circles
like
little
toys,
without
the
windup
keys
or
noise.

24

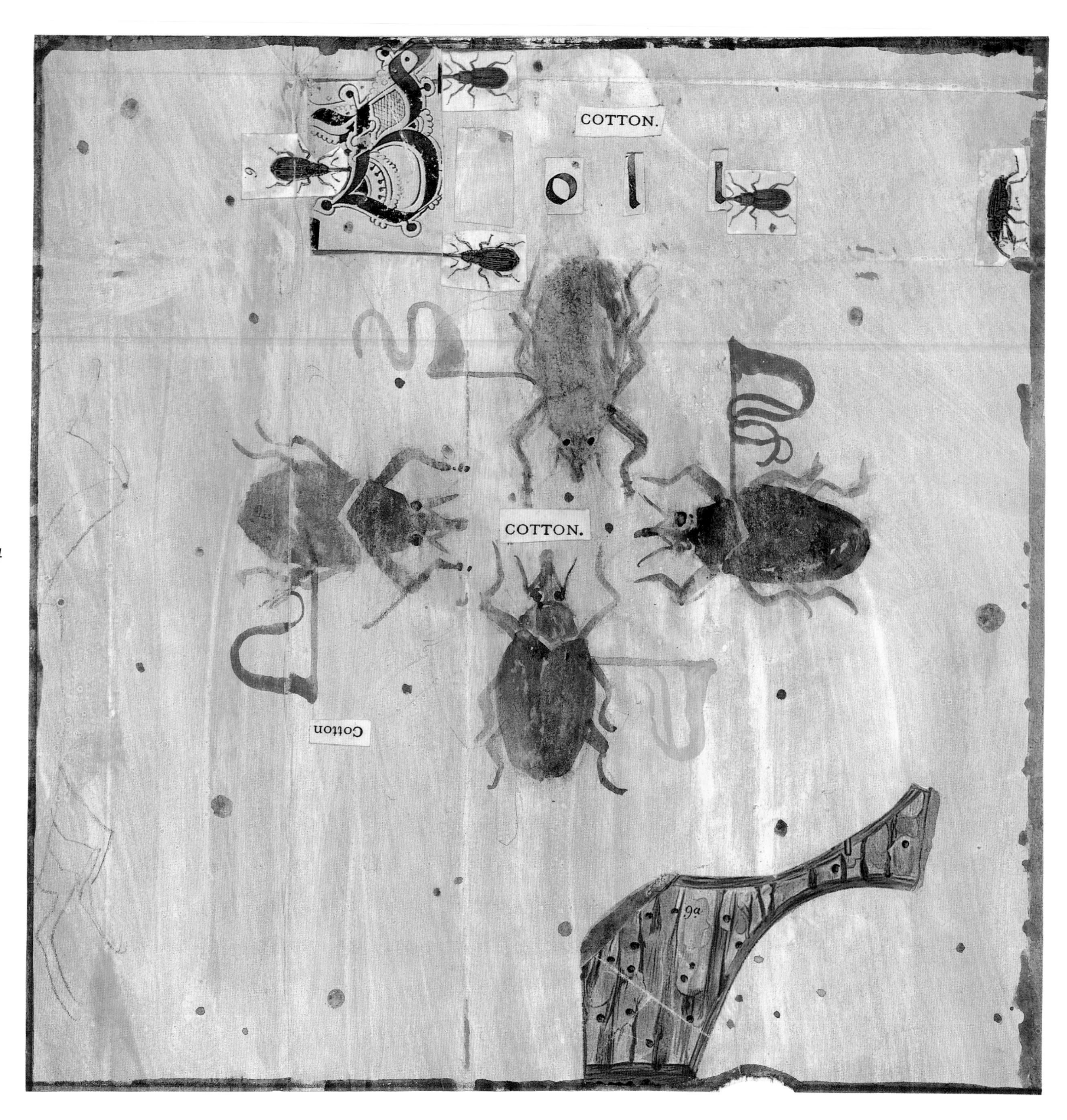

The Weevils

We are weevils.
We are evil.
We've aggrieved
Since time primeval.
With our down-curved
Beaks we bore.
Into crops
And trees we gore.
We are ruinous.
We are rotten.
We drill holes
In bolls of cotton.
We're not modern,
We're medieval.
We are weevils.
We are evil.

The Walkingstick

The walkingstick is thin, not thick,
And has a disappearing trick:
By looking like a twig or stalk,
It lives another day to walk.

The Hornet

A hornet's born with yellow rings
Ending in a point that stings.
She builds a pulpy paper nest,
In which few choose to be a guest.
A hornet is an insect killer—
She feeds her babies caterpillars,
Spiders, flies, and if she's able,
Pudding from your picnic table.

The Treehoppers

They're hip.
They hop
On top of trees.
They skip
On tips
Of twigs
With ease.
They lunge.
They plunge.
They lurch.
They lope.
Imagine what
They'd do
With rope!

H
O
P

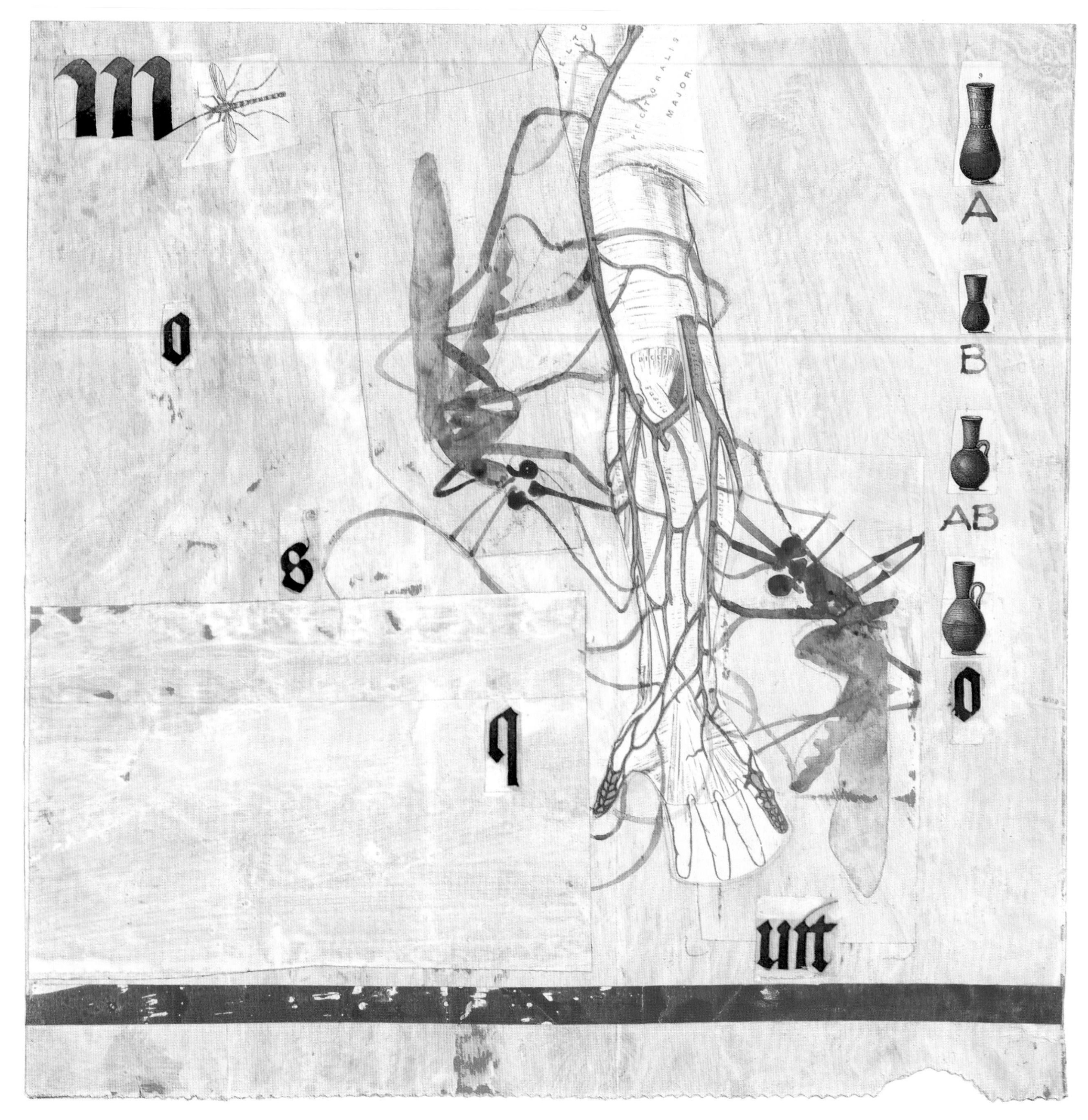
PECTORALIS MAJOR.
A
B
AB
O

The Mosquitoes

Mosquitoes are thin.
Mosquitoes are rude.
They feast on your skin
For take-out food.

The Monarch Butterfly

He is a monarch.
He is a king.
He flies great migrations.
Past nations he wings.
He is a monarch.
He is a prince.
When blackbirds attack him,
From poison they wince.
He is a monarch.
He is a duke.
Swallows that swallow him
Frequently puke.

prince

Dad

The Giant Water Bug

The giant water bug can lug
His eggs upon his back.
He gives them extra care up there
And guards them from attack.
The mother glues them to the dad,
And on his back they stay.
But does he ever get a card
Or gift for Father's Day?

The Termites

Our
high and
mighty
termite
mound
arises
far above
the ground,
and just as
deep, grows
underground.
Our nest is
blessed to be
immense. It gives
us all a firm
defense, superior
to any fence. It
shields us from our
enemies. It keeps us
cooler, by degrees.
From floods and droughts
it guarantees. A prize
nobody will assign in
architectural design, but
still our hill suits us just fine.

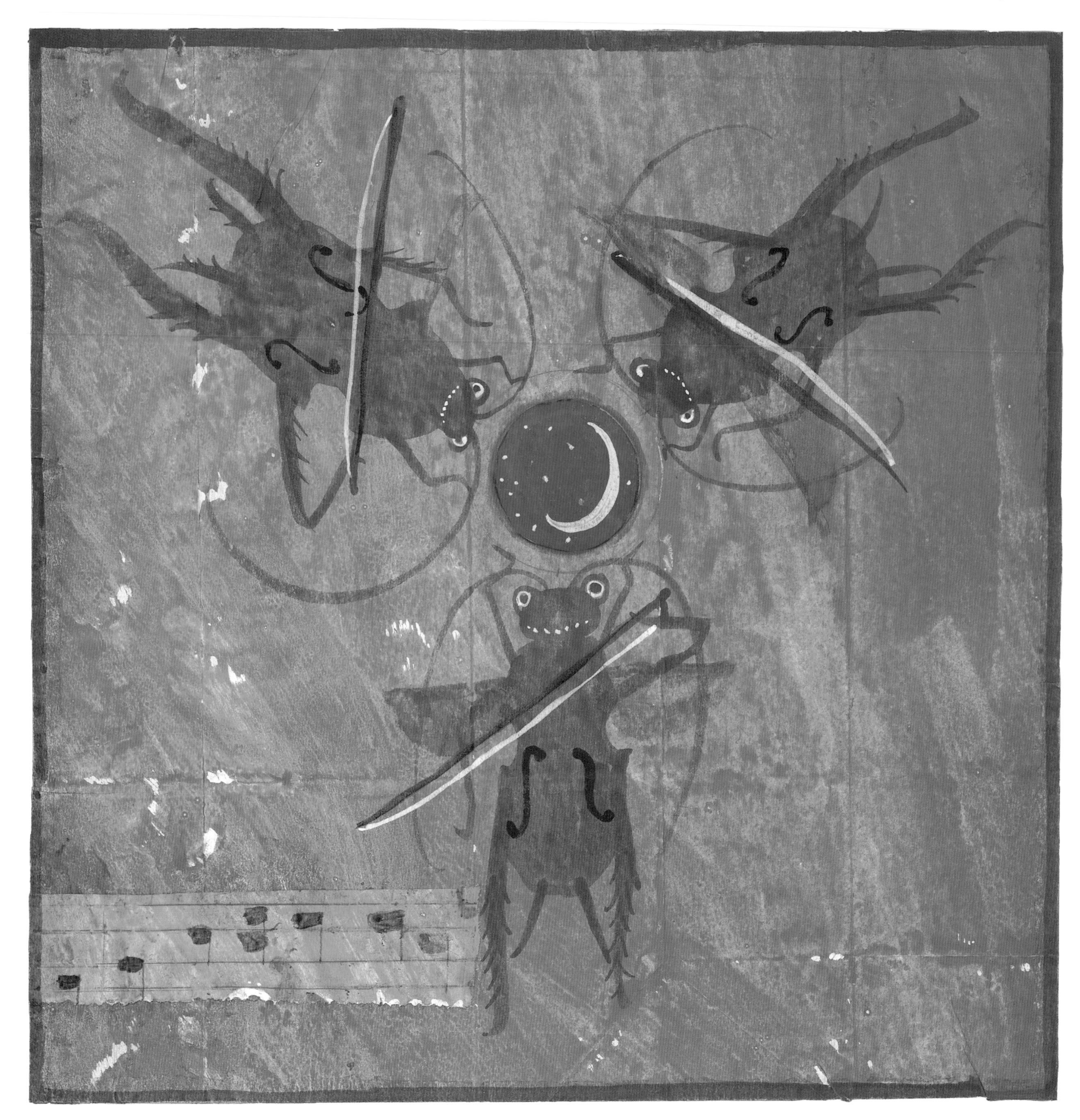

The Crickets

You don't need tickets
To listen to crickets.
They chirp and cheep for free.
They fiddle and sing
By rubbing each wing,
And never will charge you a fee.

The Locusts

Hocus-
        pocus
We are locusts.
On your farm
We swarm,
We focus.
We choose to chew
Your grain,
Your grass.
They disappear
Each time we pass.

HOCUS POCUS

The Ticks

Not gigan-tic.
Not roman-tic.
Not artis-tic.
Not majes-tic.
Not magne-tic.
Nor aesthe-tic.
Ticks are strictly parasi-tic.

The Mayfly

A mayfly flies
In May or June.
Its life is over
Far too soon.
A day or two
To dance,
To fly—
Hello
Hello
Good-bye
Good-bye.

M A Y
J U N E

The illustrations in this book were done in watercolor on
primed brown paper bags with collage.
The display type was set in Mason Alternate and Regular.
The text type was set in Sabon.
Color separations by Bright Arts, Ltd., Hong Kong
Manufactured by South China Printing Company, Ltd., China
Production supervision by Sandra Grebenar and Wendi Taylor
Designed by Kaelin Chappell

BALDWIN PUBLIC LIBRARY
3 1115 00562 2492

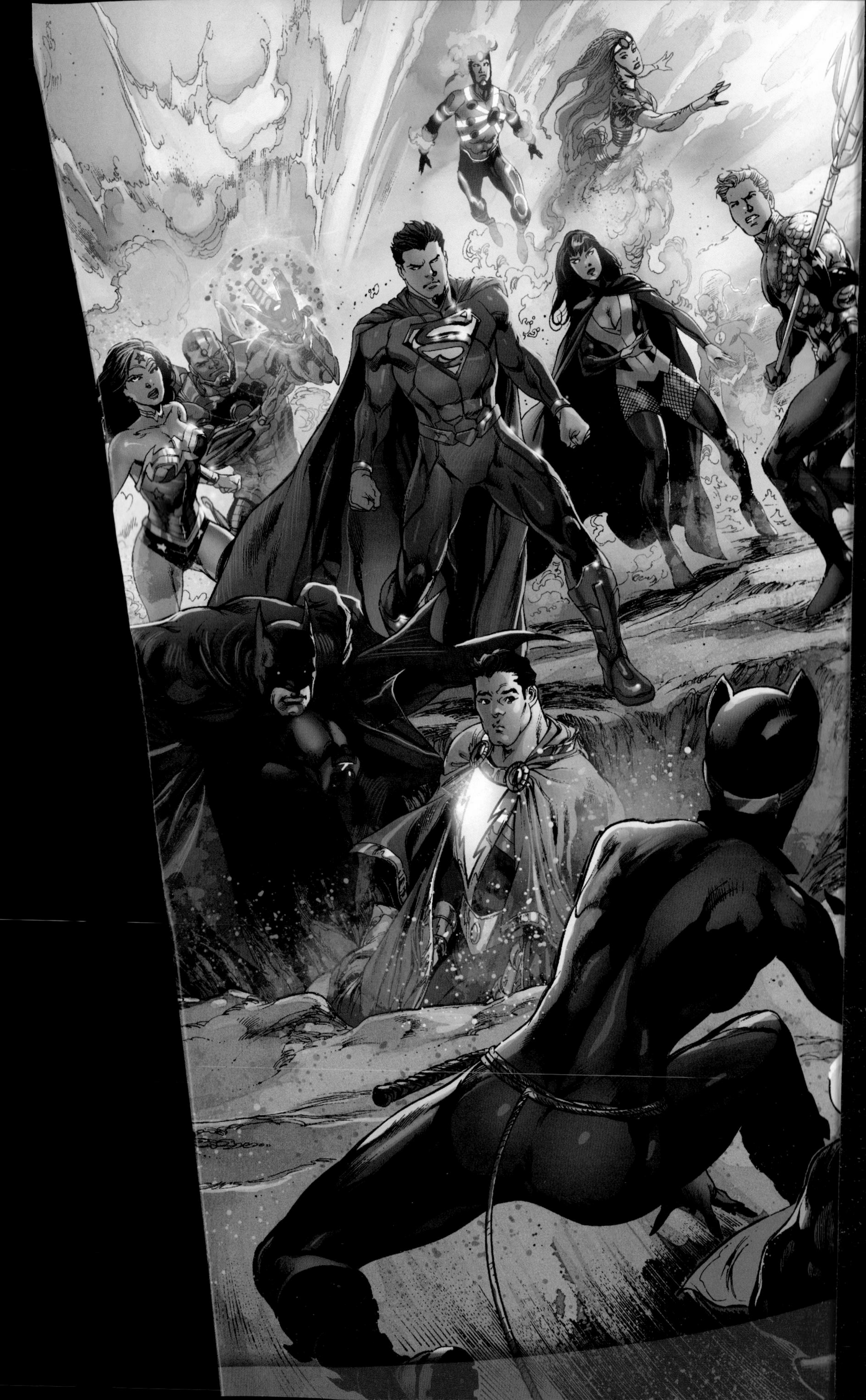

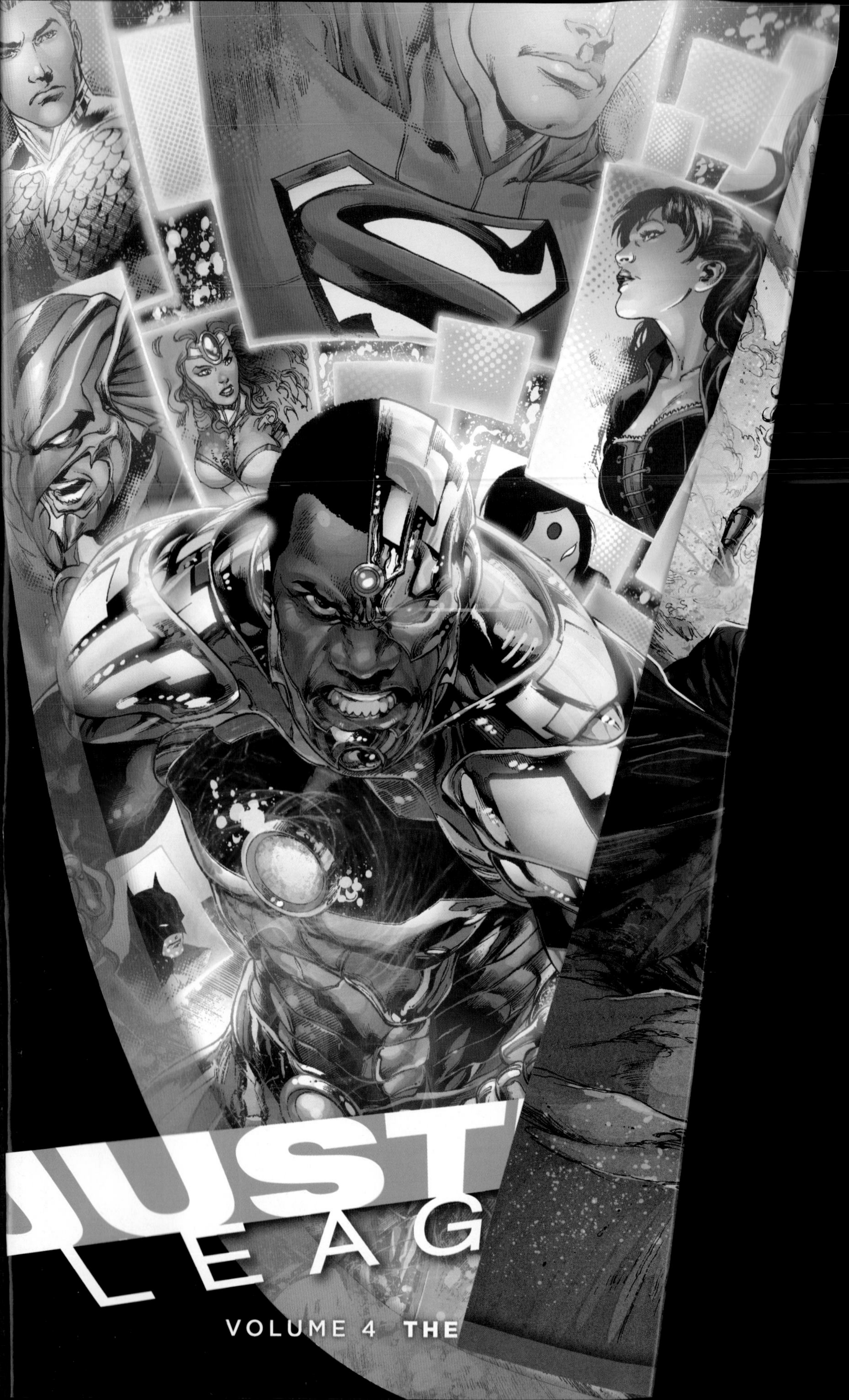
JUST
LEAG
VOLUME 4 THE

JUSTICE LEAGUE

VOLUME 4
THE GRID

GEOFF **JOHNS** writer

IVAN **REIS** JOE **PRADO** JESUS **SAIZ** OCLAIR **ALBERT**
JONATHAN **GLAPION** ZANDER **CANNON** GENE **HA**
ANDRES **GUINALDO** ROB **HUNTER** EBER **FERRIERA** artists

ROD **REIS** JEROMY **COX** ART **LYONS** **HI-FI** colorists

DEZI **SIENTY** NICK J. **NAPOLITANO** letterers

IVAN **REIS**, JOE **PRADO** & ROD **REIS**
collection cover artists

BRIAN CUNNINGHAM Editor - Original Series KATIE KUBERT Associate Editor - Original Series
KATE STEWART Assistant Editor - Original Series ROBIN WILDMAN Editor
ROBBIN BROSTERMAN Design Director - Books ROBBIE BIEDERMAN Publication Design

BOB HARRAS Senior VP - Editor-in-Chief, DC Comics

DIANE NELSON President DAN DIDIO and JIM LEE Co-Publishers
GEOFF JOHNS Chief Creative Officer
JOHN ROOD Executive VP - Sales, Marketing and Business Development
AMY GENKINS Senior VP - Business and Legal Affairs NAIRI GARDINER Senior VP - Finance
JEFF BOISON VP - Publishing Planning MARK CHIARELLO VP - Art Direction and Design
JOHN CUNNINGHAM VP - Marketing TERRI CUNNINGHAM VP - Editorial Administration
ALISON GILL Senior VP - Manufacturing and Operations HANK KANALZ Senior VP - Vertigo and Integrated Publishing
JAY KOGAN VP - Business and Legal Affairs, Publishing JACK MAHAN VP - Business Affairs, Talent
NICK NAPOLITANO VP - Manufacturing Administration SUE POHJA VP - Book Sales
COURTNEY SIMMONS Senior VP - Publicity BOB WAYNE Senior VP - Sales

JUSTICE LEAGUE VOLUME 4: THE GRID

DC Comics, 1700 Broadway, New York, NY 10019
A Warner Bros. Entertainment Company.
Printed by RR Donnelley, Salem, VA, USA. 2/28/14. First Printing.

SC ISBN: 978-1-4012-5008-9
HC ISBN: 978-1-4012-4717-1

Library of Congress Cataloging-in-Publication Data

Johns, Geoff, 1973- author.
Justice League. Volume 4, The Grid / Geoff Johns ; [illustrated by] Ivan Reis.
pages cm. — (The New 52!)
ISBN 978-1-4012-4717-1 (hardback)
1. Graphic novels. I. Reis, Ivan, illustrator. II. Title. III. Title: Grid.
PN6728.J87J6543 2014
741.5'973—dc23
2013049803

SUSTAINABLE Certified Chain of Custody

THE GRID

GEOFF JOHNS writer **JESUS SAIZ** artist **JEROMY COX** colorist **IVAN REIS, JOE PRADO** and **ROD REIS** cover artists

PITTSBURGH HIGH.
IF WE'RE GOING TO GET INTO THE SAME COLLEGE SO WE CAN KEEP UP OUR CAREER AS FIRESTORM, YOU NEED TO GET YOUR GRADES UP.
RIGHT, JASON. TOTALLY RIGHT.
BUT...I'VE SPENT MOST OF THE AFTERNOON TUTORING YOU ON MATH AND I, UM, WELL, I THOUGHT MAYBE YOU COULD TUTOR ME ON SOMETHING.
YOU KNOW BLYTHE BONNER, RIGHT?
WE'RE WORKING ON THIS PROJECT TOGETHER FOR THE COMPUTER SCIENCE FAIR, WHICH BY THE WAY YOU HAVE TO SHOW UP FOR.
I THOUGHT MAYBE SHE AND I WOULD HIT IT OFF, UH, SOCIALLY, SO I NEED YOUR ADVICE FOR ONCE.
I WANT TO ASK HER OUT.
UM. SURE. SOUNDS GOOD. TOTALLY GREAT, JACE.
WHAT?
I KNEW IT!
YOU'RE LISTENING TO THE GAME, AREN'T YOU?
HEY!
FOR TWO REASONS: ONE--BECAUSE IT'S THE PLAYOFFS, AND "B"--BECAUSE YOU'RE SO BORING.
YOU DON'T GET THE MINIMUM TEST SCORES AND I'M GOING TO BE STUCK FOLLOWING YOU TO COMMUNITY COLLEGE.
THERE'S NOTHING WRONG WITH COMMUNITY COLLEGE.
THERE IS IF YOU WANT TO BE A PHYSICIST.
WE CAN HELP YOU, JASON.
VEET
YOU SEE THAT?
WE CAN HELP YOU TOO, RONNIE.
IF YOU HELP US.

BALTIMORE.
YOUR CRY IS A WASTE OF BREATH, CANARY.
SNAKES DON'T HAVE EARS.
FWAAASHH
AAHH!
KRAK
WAS THAT YOU, BATGIRL?
WHAT HAPPENED?
OKAY, UH...
A BILLBOARD JUST HELPED ME TAKE OUT COPPERHEAD.
HELLO
AND NOW IT'S TALKING TO ME.
BLA K CANARY

SAN FRANCISCO.
I HOPE YOU HAD AS MUCH FUN AS I DID, LADIES AND GENTLEMEN!
WELL, WHAT DO YOU EXPECT, JOHN?
GREAT SHOW, ZEE!
YES, I'M MAD.
YOU TELL ME THE JUSTICE LEAGUE DARK--WELL, THAT'S WHAT THEY CALL US--YOU TELL ME THAT THIS TEAM, EXCUSE ME, YOUR TEAM NO LONGER REQUIRES MY SERVICES WITHOUT ANY EXPLANATION.
I'M TIRED OF YOU TREATING EVERYONE, ESPECIALLY ME, LIKE PAWNS IN YOUR TWISTED GAME OF LIFE.
NO. I DON'T WANT TO TALK ABOUT THIS IN PERSON.
VEET
HANG UP ON HIM, ZATANNA.
WE HAVE A PLACE FOR YOU.
NOW THAT'S SOME TRICK.

Aquaman
Batman
Cyborg
The Flash
Superman
Wonder Woman

ALL RIGHT, GUYS-- ATTACK!!

I WILL KILL ALL OF YOU, HUMANS!
BUT FIRST-- YOU
WILL
SUFFER!

RETINAL SCAN COMPLETE AND ACCEPTED.
"I'LL KILL YOU!"

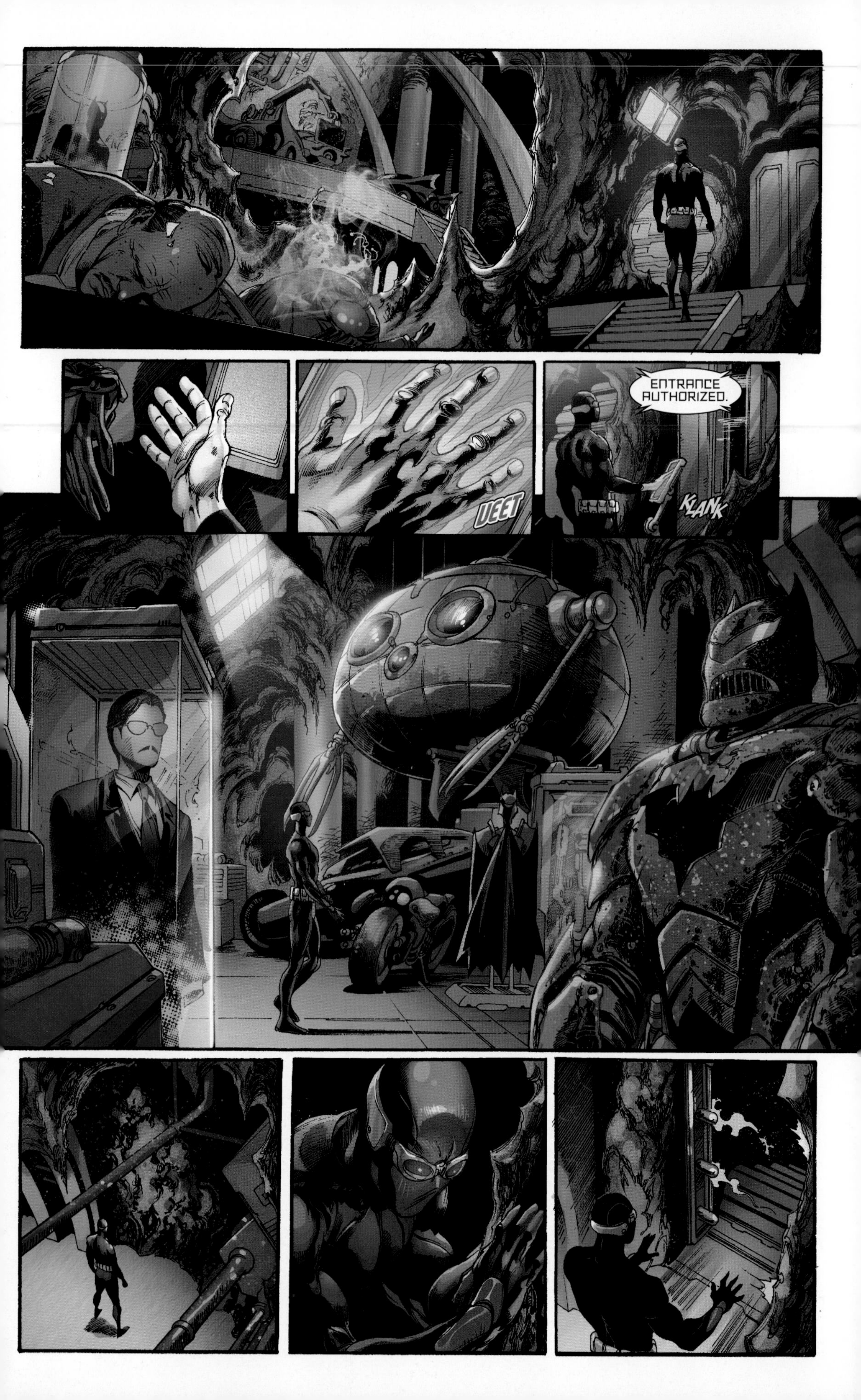
ENTRANCE AUTHORIZED.
VEET
KLANK

WHO ARE YOU?
HOW DID YOU GET IN--?
JASON?!
KK!
HN.
WHOEVER YOU ARE, BATMAN WILL FIND YOU.
I WOULD HOPE SO.
KRAKSH

BRUCE ISN'T GOING TO LIKE THIS.
HE DIDN'T LIKE IT WHEN I PUT YOUR UNIFORM UP EITHER, JASON, BUT I DON'T WANT HIM TO SIMPLY BURY THE PAIN AND SHUT HIMSELF OFF FROM EVERYONE.
THIS IS DIFFERENT. DAMIAN DIED, ALFRED. BATMAN'S SON DIED.
I WAS JUST ANOTHER ROBIN.
THAT'S YOUR PROBLEM, JASON. YOU STILL SEE YOURSELF AS "ANOTHER" ROBIN--
--BUT YOU WERE AS MUCH A SON TO BRUCE AS DAMIAN WAS. YOU WERE AS MUCH A SON TO ME. WHEN WE THOUGHT THE JOKER KILLED YOU... WE WERE ALL...
...HE WAS SO YOUNG.
...OH, GOD...
ALFRED...
YOU NEED TO, I DON'T KNOW, HAVE SOME TEA OR SOMETHING. GET SOME REST, OKAY?
LOOK...
...I'M GOING TO MISS HIM TOO.
KRRAKKZZZZTTTTT

WAR GAMES

GEOFF JOHNS writer **IVAN REIS** penciller **JOE PRADO, OCLAIR ALBERT** and **JONATHAN GLAPION** inkers
ROD REIS colorist **IVAN REIS, JOE PRADO** and **ROD REIS** cover artists

HAVE A NICE DAY
LOOKS LIKE SOME-ONE'S PLAYING MY OWN GAME *AGAINST* US.

THE ATOM'S REAL NAME IS RHONDA PINEDA.
I INVITED HER, BUT I WASN'T SURE SHE'D SHOW. SHE'S A LITTLE SHY.
WHO IS SHE?
AN UNSUNG HERO.
SOMETHING SHUT DOWN ONE OF ATLANTIS'S BOMBS IN BOSTON, FLASH. IT TOOK ME A FEW DAYS TO SORT THROUGH THE SECURITY CAMERAS AND THE SAT FEEDS. I DIDN'T EVEN SEE HER AT FIRST.
BUT SHE WAS THERE ON THE BATTLEFIELD WITH US.
"I TRACKED HER DOWN AT IVY UNIVERSITY."
THANKS FOR THE HELP IN BOSTON.
THE ATOM...
...ELEMENT WOMAN...
...AND FIRESTORM.
THAT ROBOT LADY WAS WAY OUT OF CONTROL. THAT'S THE LAST TIME WE DO THAT MAGNUS ANY FAVORS.
THERE'S NOT A WHOLE LOT OF EXPERIENCE WITH THESE THREE, BUT THEY'RE READY TO COMMIT TO THE LEAGUE FULL TIME.
VFSTKSSSHHH
OUR MONITORS ARE OUT. SOMETHING'S WRONG.
WHAT IS IT, VIC?
DURING THE FIGHT WITH PLATINUM, SOMEONE SENT EVERY ONE OF OUR CASE FILES FROM OUR SECURE SERVER TO EARTH. OUR ENTIRE FIVE-YEAR HISTORY WAS STOLEN FROM US.
WHAT? WHAT ARE YOU SAYING--?
I'M SAYING SOMEONE THAT WAS HERE HACKED OUR SYSTEM SOMEHOW, FLASH. AND THEY DIDN'T EVEN BOTHER TRYING TO COVER THEIR TRACKS.
IN FACT, THEY LEFT A MESSAGE FOR ME TO FIND.
WHAT IS IT?
BEEP

WHERE DID SHE COME FROM?
HI, GUYS.
IS IT TOO LATE FOR TRYOUTS?

I WANT TO SEE WILL.
KRK
I WANT TO GO HOME.
REMEMBER CYBORG SAID ONLY THE PLATINUM BODY CHANGES-- THERE'S SOMETHING DELICATE INSIDE THAT WE HAVE TO PROTECT.
DO NOT SCREW THIS UP, RONNIE.
JUST MAKE SURE I DON'T.
PLATINUM TO WATER--COMIN' RIGHT UP!
FFZZZAMMM
THAT'S IT.
JUST A LITTLE MORE.
WAIT--!
I LIKED HER.
THE RESPONSOMETER! IT'S GOING TO--

HER OUTER BODY--THE PLATINUM--IF THERE'S A WAY TO SEPARATE IT FROM THE RESPONSOMETER--
I HAVE AN IDEA.
FIRESTORM!
RONNIE, CYBORG'S CALLING FOR US!
HUH? YEAH?
PLATINUM, I KNOW I LOOK SCARY, BUT I'M YOUR FRIEND.
I DON'T KNOW YOU.
MY NAME IS EMILY.
HOW ACCURATE ARE YOU WITH YOUR POWERS?
ONE HUNDRED PERCENT!
I'M NOT LYING, JASON!

DOCTOR MAGNUS?! I ASSUME YOU'RE GETTING THESE READINGS DOWN THERE.
YES, CYBORG, UNFORTUNATELY. THIS MAY HAVE BEEN PREMATURE AND THE FINAL NAIL IN THE COFFIN TO PROJECT: METAL MEN. I'M SORRY. I SHOULDN'T HAVE SENT HER. I'M JUST SO DESPERATE TO--
I'M TRYING TO CONNECT WITH PLATINUM'S SYSTEM, BUT I CAN'T.
SHE'S OFF-LINE, CYBORG. I WANTED HER TO FUNCTION INDEPENDENTLY.
WHERE IS H-HE?
"WHERE IS DOCTOR WILL MAGNUS?!"
HER BODY IS MADE UP OF SOLID PLATINUM THAT'S BEING CONTROLLED AND MANIPULATED BY HER RESPONSOMETER.
HER WHAT?
HER BRAIN. IT'S EXTREMELY FRAGILE AND IF IT'S DESTROYED... I CAN'T REBUILD HER.
PLEASE. IT'S VERY IMPORTANT YOU DON'T HARM THAT DEVICE.

DADING-DA-LA-LING-DINGDING
IT CAN'T BE THAT TIME ALREADY!
IT IS!
GUYS, I'M SORRY, BUT I'VE GOT TO GO.
WHAT? YOU CAN'T LEAVE NOW!
WE'RE IN THE MIDDLE OF AN APE-ORC BATTLE!
AND WE'RE HEADING INTO THE BLACKROCK VALLEY SO ARNOLD CAN GET THE CLOAK OF BALANCE!
THE FIRE BEASTS WILL BE WAITING FOR US!
I REALLY WISH I COULD STAY, BUT I CAN'T!
AT LEAST LEAVE US THE FROST BLADE!
THIS THING TOOK ME FOREVER TO GET! I...I'M SORRY!
YOU TRAITOR!

"NOW WE'RE ALL GOING TO DIE!"
GEEZ.
WHAT A DRAMA QUEEN.
GAME SAVED.
GUILD BATTLES OFF-LINE.
GUILD BATTLES
ALL RIGHT, RHONDA, CHECK YOURSELF BEFORE YA WRECK YOURSELF. THIS IS IT. THIS IS THE BIG TIME.
THIS IS THE JUSTICE LEAGUE.
SWEET.
22,300 MILES ABOVE EARTH.
THE WATCHTOWER.
HELLO?
IS ANYONE ELSE HERE?
I AM NOT ASKING HIM TO TEACH ME THAT.

BECAUSE WHY DO WE NEED TO LEARN MARTIAL ARTS OR WHATEVER IT IS HE DOES? THAT'S BATMAN'S THING, JASON.
FIRESTORM'S ALL ABOUT PHYSICS, ELEMENTS AND ALL THAT CRAP.
YOU KNOW WHAT I MEANT.
GET MY FEET OFF THE TABLE? YOU SOUND LIKE MY MOM. AGAIN.
EMBARRASS YOU?
UM, EXCUSE ME.
WHO ARE YOU TALKING TO, FIRESTORM?
OH, UH, NO ONE IMPORTANT, ATOM.
ARE WE THE ONLY ONES HERE?
SO FAR, YEAH. IT'S JUST US.
MAYBE THEY FORGOT WE WERE SUPPOSED TO MEET TO GET OUR OFFICIAL CERTIFICATION TODAY.
I THOUGHT SUPERMAN NEVER FORGOT ANYTHING. ISN'T THAT ONE OF HIS SUPER-POWERS?
I'M NOT SURE.
WELL, WHEREVER THEY ARE--

"--I'M SURE THEY'RE DOING SOMETHING IMPORTANT."
KAHNDAQ.
...INTENSIFIED ON DAY THREE OF THE STANDOFF BETWEEN THE KAHNDAQI MILITARY AND THE SONS OF ADAM.
THE KAHNDAQ GOVERNMENT CONTINUES TO DENY REQUESTS BY THE U.S. TO ENTER THE COUNTRY AND CONFRONT THE SONS OF ADAM, THE TERRORIST GROUP RESPONSIBLE FOR THE RECENT BOMBINGS OF ITS EMBASSY IN SOUTH AFRICA.
<"THEY AREN'T GOING TO RELEASE OUR BROTHERS FROM THEIR PRISONS. THEY REFUSE TO NEGOTIATE!">
<THEN WE KILL ONE OF THE HOSTAGES TO SHOW THEM WE WON'T NEGOTIATE EITHER.>
<KAHNDAQ BELONGS IN THE HANDS OF THE SONS OF ADAM, NOT ITS PUPPETEERS!>
<GET UP!>
<HARKA, WAIT!>
<WHAT?>
<WE HAD EIGHT HOSTAGES.>
<SO?>
<WHY ARE THERE NOW TEN?>
<WHAT IS THIS?>
<WHO ARE YOU?>

AAAHHH!
<WHAT IS IT?!>
<HELP.>
<JUSTICE.>
"HE'LL NEVER CHANGE."

THE OLD MAN GETS HIS HEAD SMASHED INTO A GLASS CASE AND HE'S STILL WORRIED ABOUT MAKING US *LUNCH.*
FINALLY GOT HIM TO LIE DOWN AND TAKE A BREATHER THOUGH.
GOOD.
BRUCE, I...
I SHOULD'VE HEARD THEM COME IN.
I KNOW YOU'RE DISAPPOINTED. I'M DISAPPOINTED IN MYSELF--
JASON.
I'M JUST GLAD YOU'RE BOTH OKAY.
GO WATCH OVER ALFRED. THE LEAGUE WILL HELP ME FIND OUT WHO ATTACKED YOU BOTH.
WHOEVER IT WAS, HE WAS WEARING A SUIT THAT GAVE OFF AN *ELECTROMAGNETIC PULSE.* HE'S NOTHING BUT A *BLUR* ON THE SECURITY CAMERAS. I'VE SCANNED FOR ANY TRACE OF *DNA--*
AND, CYBORG?
THERE'S *NONE.*
COULD IT HAVE BEEN SOME KIND OF ANDROID?
PRESSURE SENSORS ON THE FLOOR INDICATE THE INTRUDER WEIGHED IN AT ONLY ABOUT 180 POUNDS.
WHOEVER IT WAS, THEY WERE PROBABLY HUMAN.

AND THERE'S NO RESIDUAL ENERGY SIGNATURE FROM ANY RECORDED TELEPORTATION DEVICE.
SO WE DON'T KNOW WHO THEY ARE OR HOW THEY GOT IN.
THEY DIDN'T GET IN THROUGH THE RIVERS.
EVEN IF THEY COULD BREATHE UNDERWATER, THE CURRENTS WOULD'VE SWEPT THEM AWAY.
HOW ABOUT WHY? THEY OBVIOUSLY KNOW WHO YOU ARE, BRUCE. THEY CAME HERE FOR SOMETHING.
BUT THEY DIDN'T ACCESS ANY COMPUTERS.
AND THEY DIDN'T SERIOUSLY INJURE ALFRED OR JASON.
SO WHAT WOULD THEY BE AFTER?
...I'M NOT SURE.
DAMN.
WHAT IS IT, VIC?
TROUBLE, I THINK.
...CONFIRMATION THAT SUPERMAN AND WONDER WOMAN CROSSED THE KAHNDAQI BORDER AND RESCUED THE HOSTAGES--
--MAKING THEM THE FIRST AMERICANS TO ENTER KAHNDAQ IN OVER TWENTY-SIX YEARS, SPARKING ACCUSATIONS AGAINST THE JUSTICE LEAGUE AND THE U.S. OF SPYING ON THE TROUBLED NATION.
LOCATE SUPERMAN AND WONDER WOMAN, CYBORG.

"AND TAKE ME THERE."
IT'S BEAUTIFUL, ISN'T IT?
IT IS.
I'VE BEEN ALL OVER THE WORLD, BUT NEVER KAHNDAQ.
THEY'VE BEEN BURIED BY VIOLENCE EVER SINCE THE U.S. TRIED TO APPOINT THEIR CHOICE OF LEADER.
THE PEOPLE REBELLED. THEN THE COUNTRY WAS DIVIDED BY CIVIL WAR. AND IT'S NEVER GOTTEN OUT.
WE COULD SAVE THEM, CLARK.
NOT JUST THE HOSTAGES, BUT THE ENTIRE COUNTRY.
IT'S NOT UP TO US TO CHANGE THE WORLD, DIANA.
WHY NOT?
I MADE THAT CHOICE A LONG TIME AGO AND IT WAS THE RIGHT CHOICE. I USE MY POWERS TO INSPIRE, NOT INTERFERE.
SOMETIMES THE WORLD NEEDS US TO INTERFERE.
WE COULD MAKE THINGS WORSE.
BY DELIVERING THE WATER THEY NEED? OR THE FOOD AND SUPPLIES THAT WOULD IMPROVE THEIR LIVES?
GOVERNMENT SANCTIONS MAY PREVENT OTHERS FROM COMING IN HERE, BUT NOT US.
NOTHING CAN STOP US, CLARK.
YOU DON'T WANT TO SAY THAT.

SUPER-VILLAINS SAY THAT, DIANA.
YOU KNOW THAT'S NOT WHAT SHE MEANT.
I DO, CLARK, BUT A LOT OF PEOPLE WOULDN'T.
HOW DID YOU GET HERE, BRUCE?
AND WITHOUT OUR HEARING YOU?
CYBORG. HE HAS A NEW SILENT MODE IN HIS RECENT UPGRADE.
I ASKED VIC TO GIVE ME SOME SPACE AND TIME WITH YOU TWO BECAUSE WE'RE GOING TO TALK ABOUT THINGS THAT MIGHT GET UNCOMFORTABLE.
YOU KICKED A HORNETS' NEST TODAY. KAHNDAQ IS THREATENING TO RETALIATE AGAINST U.S. INTERESTS.
AMERICANS HAVE BEEN BANNED FROM ENTERING KAHNDAQ FOR DECADES. THE POLITICS--
WOULD'VE COST LIVES. WE HAD NO CHOICE.
YOU DID HAVE A CHOICE, DIANA.
YOU AND CLARK COULD'VE DONE THIS QUIETLY.
WERE YOU PLANNING A STEALTH MISSION TO GO IN AND SAVE THEM?
IF YOU HAD COME TO ME WITH THIS, I WOULD HAVE. INSTEAD WE'VE GOT THE JUSTICE LEAGUE ONCE AGAIN CAUGHT IN THE PUBLIC EYE IN A BAD WAY.
THE MORE THE WORLD DISTRUSTS US, THE HARDER IT'S GOING TO BE TO GET THE JOB DONE.
IT WASN'T THE JUSTICE LEAGUE THAT CAME HERE, IT WAS DIANA AND I.

WHEN YOU AND SHE ARE TOGETHER, CLARK, YOU REPRESENT THE JUSTICE LEAGUE.
YOU CANNOT DO THIS TO US.
YOU KNOW WE'D NEVER DO ANYTHING TO PURPOSELY UPSET YOU, BRUCE. WE'RE YOUR FRIENDS.
THEN WE CAN BE HONEST WITH ONE ANOTHER, CAN'T WE, CLARK?
I KNOW YOU AND DIANA HAVE BEEN SEEING ONE ANOTHER OUTSIDE OF THE TEAM.
DOES THE REST OF THE TEAM KNOW?
NOT YET, THOUGH I'D ASSUME THEY'VE SUSPECTED SINCE YOU'VE BEEN SPENDING SO MUCH TIME WITH ONE ANOTHER.
WE CONNECTED, BRUCE. IT JUST HAPPENED.

I'M HAPPY THAT YOU BOTH...FOUND SOMETHING TOGETHER.
YOU JUST NEED TO UNDERSTAND HOW THE REST OF THE WORLD--THE WORLD WHO DOESN'T KNOW YOU LIKE *I* DO--WILL *REACT.*
YOU'RE THE *TWO MOST POWERFUL BEINGS* ON EARTH.
THEY'RE GOING TO BE GUNNING FOR YOU.
WHO WILL?
WHOEVER'S AFRAID OF WHAT YOU TWO COULD DO.
"SOMEONE BROKE INTO THE BATCAVE LAST NIGHT.
"AND THEY DIDN'T DO IT TO GET AT *ME,* SUPERMAN.
"THEY DID IT TO GET TO *YOU.*"
WHAT'S IN THE BATCAVE THAT CAN HURT CLARK?
WHAT DID YOU *DO,* BRUCE?
"AREN'T YOU WORRIED?"

WE REALLY SHOULDN'T BE *EXPLORING* ON OUR OWN, FIRESTORM.
NO, SHE'S *NOT* RIGHT.
UM, WHAT?
LOOK, WE'VE BEEN WAITING ALMOST AN *HOUR* AND I'M *STARVING.* IF I COULD TRANSMUTE ELEMENTS INTO ORGANICS I'D ZAP ME UP A *PIZZA,* BUT I *CAN'T* SO I NEED TO FIND FOOD THE OLD-FASHIONED WAY--
--IN A *KITCHEN.*
ARE YOU SURE THERE'S A KITCHEN IN HERE? I HAVEN'T EVEN SEEN A BATHROOM.
OH! CAN YOU TRANSMUTE ONE OF THESE CLOSETS INTO A BATHROOM?
WHAT COLOR DO YOU WANT THE WALLPAPER?
PERIMETER DEFENSES OFF-LINE.
YOU HEAR THAT? THE JUSTICE LEAGUE MUST BE BACK!
ATOM? ARE YOU ALL RIGHT?
KRAAAANKKKK
WHO ARE YOU?

AND WHERE IS THE JUSTICE LEAGUE?
TELL ME NOW OR I WILL TEAR IT FROM YOUR MINDS--
--BEFORE I FEAST ON YOUR FLESH.

SECRETS

GEOFF JOHNS writer **ZANDER CANNON** layouts **GENE HA, ANDRES GUINALDO** and **JOE PRADO** pencillers

GENE HA, ROB HUNTER and **JOE PRADO** inkers **ART LYONS** and **HI-FI** colorists **IVAN REIS, JOE PRADO** and **ROD REIS** cover artists

BIG BELLY
I'M NOT WHO YOU THINK I AM.
WELCOME TO BIG BELLY BURGER!
24HR DRIVE THRU
I WONDER IF SHE'S WHO THEY THINK SHE IS. THEY'VE HAD ME WATCH HER ALL WEEK.
WOULD YOU LIKE TO TRY OUR NEW STRAWBERRY-BANANA TWISTER SHAKE TODAY?
I LOVE MIXING FLAVORS!
GIVE ME NINE OF THOSE! UM, EIGHT CHICKEN SLIDER COMBOS, PLEASE! AND A FISH SANDWICH FOR ARTHUR, I THINK!
THAT'LL BE $54.82. PLEASE PULL UP TO THE SECOND WINDOW.
HER REAL NAME IS EMILY SUNG.
BUT SHE'S GONE BY A DIFFERENT NAME EVER SINCE THE ACCIDENT.
HI! I'M ELEMENT WOMAN
I'M THE NEWEST MEMBER OF THE JUSTICE LEAGUE!
I GUESS THEY LIKE ME.
대에서 탈출했다!
OR.
AT LEAST I HOPE THEY DO.
SINCE THE ACCIDENT, EMILY'S BEEN ABLE TO METAMORPHOSE HERSELF INTO ANY ELEMENT FOUND IN THE HUMAN BODY.
SHE'S ALSO INCAPABLE OF LOOKING HUMAN. IN FACT, THIS IS AS CLOSE AS SHE CAN GET. SKIN LIKE CHALK. HAIR LIKE SILLY STRING. VOICE LIKE A CARTOON.
I'M NOT SURE IF HER ABILITIES MADE EMILY MENTALLY UNSTABLE, OR IF SHE WAS A FEW ELEMENTS SHY OF THE PERIODIC TABLE TO BEGIN WITH.

FIVE SECONDS AGO, ELEMENT WOMAN USED THE TELEPORTATION SYSTEM TO TRANSPORT UP TO THE JUSTICE LEAGUE'S WATCHTOWER SATELLITE.
SHE BROUGHT TWO BAGS OF FAST FOOD WITH HER.
I'M GUESSING SHE'S THE FIRST PERSON IN HISTORY TO BRING THE JUSTICE LEAGUE SHAKES. IT'S THE LITTLE THINGS THAT SAY THE MOST ABOUT SOMEONE.
IT'S THE LITTLE THINGS THAT MATTER.
WHO ARE YOU?!
WHERE ARE THE JUSTICE LEAGUE?!
BIG BELLY BURGERS
IF ELEMENT WOMAN IS RECRUIT NUMBER ONE, I'M RECRUIT NUMBER TWO.

RECRUIT NUMBER THREE IS
FIRESTORM
AND TECHNICALLY, HE'S RECRUIT NUMBERS THREE AND FOUR.
BEHIND THE POWERS, FIRESTORM IS ACTUALLY TWO HIGH SCHOOL STUDENTS. A JOCK NAMED RONNIE RAYMOND AND AN HONOR STUDENT NAMED JASON RUSCH.
MY NAME IS RHONDA PINEDA, BUT THEY CALL ME
THE ATOM.
WHEN THESE TWO BOND TOGETHER, THEY CAN FLY, MANIPULATE ENERGY AND TRANSMUTE ANY INORGANIC ELEMENT INTO ANOTHER.
THEY FORM THE MOST DANGEROUS SUPER-HUMAN IN THE WORLD.
THAT'S A SECRET.
I HAVE A SECRET TOO.

WE WERE SUPPOSED TO MEET THE JUSTICE LEAGUE HERE FOR AN OFFICIAL INDUCTION CEREMONY. SOMETHING I WAS DREADING, TRUTH BE TOLD.
THE TRUTH.
I'VE ALMOST FORGOTTEN HOW TO TELL THE TRUTH.
WHERE IS SUPERMAN?
HEY! THAT WAS SUPERMAN'S LUNCH!
YOU DIDN'T HAPPEN TO SEE SUPERMAN, DID YOU, ELEMENT WOMAN?
I SAW HIM SUNDAY, ATOM! THE DAY WE MET!
I KNOW THAT. I MEANT ON YOUR WAY UP HERE.
I NEED THE STRONGEST ELEMENT YOU CAN THINK OF, JASON.
TITANIUM, RONNIE.
FZZAMM
OKAY, GALS! I SEALED OFF THE BREACH AND MADE A VAULT DOOR, BUT IT'S NOT GOING TO KEEP DESPERO OUT OF HERE FOREVER.
NO, WE'RE NOT EQUIPPED FOR THIS, JASON.
MY NAME'S EMILY, FIRESTORM, BUT I AGREE.
I'M NOT SURE WHAT TO DO NEXT. I CAN'T KEEP TURNING THE AIR INTO METAL UP HERE. WITH THE SYSTEMS DOWN, OUR OXYGEN'S LIMITED.
YOU COULD BREATHE ME IF YOU NEED TO.
THAT'S KINDA CREEPY, EM. I SAY WE FIND THE EXIT DOOR AND--
WE CAN'T LEAVE. WE NEED TO STAND OUR GROUND.
STAND OUR GROUND? AGAINST DESPERO? YOU HAVE HEARD OF DESPERO, HAVEN'T YOU, ATOM?
I'VE READ THE FILES ON EVERY ENEMY OF THE JUSTICE LEAGUE.
HE WAS ONE OF THE FIRST ALIENS THE LEAGUE EVER TOOK ON.
YEAH! HE WAS THE RULER OF LIKE, THREE PLANETS BEFORE THE LEAGUE KICKED HIM OFF HIS THRONE. AND THE LAST TIME THEY FOUGHT, THEY BARELY BEAT HIM--AND THAT WAS WHEN MARTIAN MANHUNTER WAS ON THE TEAM!
WELL, WE'RE WHAT THE LEAGUE'S GOT NOW.
I SAY WE LET DESPERO IN AND WE TAKE HIM ON.

LET HIM IN? AS IF WE HAVE A CHOICE.
BOOM
YEAH, I HEARD HER, JASON.
"WE'RE JUSTICE LEAGUERS--SO LET'S ACT LIKE IT." THANKS FOR THE PEP TALK.
ZEE
ZEE
ZEE
BOOOMM
BOOOMM
BOOOMM
THIS COULD BE USED TO MY ADVANTAGE.
IF DESPERO DOESN'T KILL US.
KRNCH
THINK FAST, JASON!
THOOOO
YEAH, THAT'LL WORK!

FZZAMM
ONE SNOWSTORM COMIN' UP!
SNOW?! I MISS CHRISTMAS!
YOU AND FIRESTORM KEEP DISTRACTING HIM, EMILY.
MAYBE I CAN GET IN HIS HEAD AND TRIGGER AN ANEURYSM.
MY MIND ISN'T AS FALLIBLE AS OTHERS YOU MAY HAVE ENCOUN-TERED, ATOM.
OTHERS AS WEAK AS YOUR ALLIES HERE.
YES.
I CAN HEAR YOU ARGUING IN THERE, FIRESTORM.
AAHHH!
YOUR PSYCHIC BOND IS WHAT ALLOWS YOU TO TAKE APART ATOMS.
BUT THAT BOND IS ONLY AS STRONG AS YOUR RELATIONSHIP.

SO THAT BOND CAN EASILY BE BROKEN!
ZZZAMMFF
AHHH!
R-RONNIE?!
FIRESTORM?!
HE'S LIKE TWO PEOPLE!
MARTIAN MANHUNTER COULD BARELY BEAT DESPERO.
MAYBE I WAS WRONG.
DAMMIT... WHERE ARE THEY, ANYWAY?

WHERE ARE THE JUSTICE LEAGUE?
YOU HAD A KRYPTONITE RING IN THE BATCAVE THAT WAS STOLEN?
BY SOMEONE WHO OBVIOUSLY KNOWS MY IDENTITY, DIANA.
AND THEY KNEW I HAD THE RING. THEY WENT RIGHT TO IT.
WHAT WERE YOU DOING WITH KRYPTONITE, BRUCE?
I GAVE IT TO HIM, DIANA.
"YOU GAVE IT TO HIM, CLARK?"
WE HAVE TO FIND OUT WHO BROKE INTO THE BATCAVE.
GUYS!
WE'VE GOT MAJOR PROBLEMS WITH THE WATCHTOWER.
THE DEFENSE SYSTEMS ARE OFF.
YOUR PSYCHE IS ABNORMAL AND SPLINTERED AND LESS VULNERABLE TO ME THAN OTHER HUMANS.
ELEMENT WOMAN'S ROTATING THROUGH ELEMENTS, LOOKING FOR SOMETHING DESPERO CAN'T BREAK.

BUT YOUR BODY IS STILL FRAGILE.
SHE DOESN'T FIND ANYTHING.
WE NEED HELP.
PORT US UP THERE.
I CAN'T.
WHY NOT?
THE COORDINATES KEEP CHANGING.
ACQUIRING SIGNAL
"THE WATCHTOWER IS FALLING TO EARTH!"
YOUR MIND IS A MYSTERY, LITTLE ONE.
I CAN'T LET HIM IN. I CAN'T LET HIM SEE IT.
ARE THE PATHWAYS TOO SMALL TO READ?
NO...I CAN SEE IT.
YOU ARE HIDING SOMETHING--
DESPERO!
RRARRRR!
IT'S EXACTLY WHAT THEY KEEP TELLING ME. YOU SAY HIS NAME AND HE ALWAYS SHOWS UP.

J'ONN J'ONZZ-- THE LAST OF THE MANHUNTERS FROM MARS.
YOU SHOULD HAVE STAYED IN YOUR PRISON, DESPERO. IT WAS SAFER.
FOR YOU.
STAY ON MARS?
YOUR DEAD WORLD HAS NOTHING TO OFFER ME, J'ONN.
DESPERO NEARLY READ MY THOUGHTS. I CAN'T RISK GROWING ANY BIGGER.

I CAME HERE TO RIP APART THE JUSTICE LEAGUE.
I HAD HOPED YOU'D BE THE LAST I WOULD HAVE MY REVENGE UPON.
YOU WHO BETRAYED HIS BROTHER!
AS LONG AS I'M THIS SIZE I'M INSULATED FROM DESPERO'S TELEPATHY.
AND MANHUNTER'S.
THE WATCHTOWER'S GOING TO LAND RIGHT ON THE EAST COAST.
YOU'RE THE ONLY ONE WHO MIGHT BE ABLE TO STOP THAT FROM HAPPENING, SUPERMAN. IF YOU CAN'T--
I CAN, VIC.
"THAT'S WHAT I DO."
BROTHERS?!
WE ARE NOT BROTHERS, DESPERO.
EARTH WOULD SAY DIFFERENT, J'ONN. THEY SEE US BOTH AS "ALIENS" INVADING THEIR WORLD.
YOU TRIED TO ENSLAVE THEM.
AND WHAT ARE YOU DOING TO THEM, J'ONN?
I KNOW. YOU ASKED ME TO BE A PART OF IT.
YET, NOW YOU DEFEND THEM? THOSE THAT KILLED YOUR WORLD?
A WORLD YOU LET DIE!
YOU LET MARS BURN!

AND MARS WILL FOREVER SMOLDER WITH THE FIRE OF YOUR FAILURE!
WE COULD HAVE RULED GALAXIES TOGETHER, J'ONN.
INSTEAD, YOU WASTE YOUR POWER ON PROTECTING THE WEAK.
IT IS A THANKLESS EXISTENCE.
KRNCHH
IT IS FINALLY DONE.
GOOD-BYE, J'ONN.

DESPERO!
YOU BRING ME TO A CONSTRUCTION OF MARS AND BELIEVE ME SHATTERED BY ITS IMAGERY AND METAPHOR?
YOU MISTAKE ME FOR THOSE LIKE SUPERMAN AND THE GREEN LANTERN.
YOU MISTAKE ME FOR SOMEONE SENTIMENTAL.
I AM THE MARTIAN MANHUNTER.
THE LAST TIME WE FACED, I ABIDED BY THE JUSTICE LEAGUE'S RULES.
I LIMITED THE USE OF MY TELEPATHY.
BUT THIS TIME YOUR MIND IS MINE TO WALK INTO.
AARR!
IT IS MINE TO PLAY WITH.

MINE TO BREAK.
RRRARARRHH!
EVERY LIGHT IN THE WATCHTOWER GOES OUT.
THEN IT GOES SILENT.
UNTIL THE SOUND OF SOMETHING HITTING METAL ECHOES THROUGH THE HALLS.

ARE YOU ALL RIGHT, ATOM?
I THINK SO, YES. WHAT DID YOU DO TO HIM?
I REVERSED THE FLOW OF HIS SYNAPSES.
IT WILL TAKE DAYS, MAYBE WEEKS, FOR HIS MIND TO RECOVER.
TELL NO ONE I WAS HERE.
YIKES.
I HEAR MY NEW TEAMMATES RE-FORM THEMSELVES.
THEY DIDN'T SEE HIM, DID THEY?
RRANNNNK
EVERYONE ALL RIGHT?
SUPERMAN?

I DON'T KNOW WHAT TO SAY.
DESPERO? ATOM?
UH...HI, SUPERMAN?
DID YOU HANDLE HIM YOURSELF?
SO I LIE.
KINDA?
THAT'S-- NNN!
SUPERMAN? WHAT'S WRONG?
SUPERMAN?!
"WE'RE LUCKY WE GOT HIM OUT OF THERE AS SOON AS WE DID."
THIS IS KRYPTONITE.

IS SUPERMAN GOING TO BE OKAY?
HE FLEW TO THE SUN TO RECHARGE, ELEMENT WOMAN. HE SHOULD BE FINE BY DAWN.
WHERE ARE WE, ANYWAY?
HAPPY HARBOR, RHODE ISLAND. WE NEED TO SALVAGE WHAT WE CAN FROM THE WATCHTOWER. WE'LL MOVE IT INTO THAT CAVE FOR NOW--
WHERE DID DESPERO GET KRYPTONITE?
FROM ME, ARTHUR.
FROM YOU?
I HAD SOME BACK IN GOTHAM. I'VE BEEN STUDYING IT...
...IN HOPES OF FINDING A CURE FOR SUPERMAN.
I COULD HELP YOU. I KNOW A LOT ABOUT ELEMENTS.
AND I'D LIKE TO HELP TOO, BATMAN.
I CAN SEE THINGS IN A WAY NO ONE ELSE CAN.
THOUGH KRYPTONITE LOOKS PRETTY COMPLICATED.
DESPERO WASN'T THE ONE WHO BROKE INTO THE BATCAVE, BATMAN. THE BLUR ON THE SECURITY CAMERAS WAS THE SIZE OF A HUMAN.
SOMEONE GAVE THE KRYPTONITE TO DESPERO.
AND UNLEASHED HIM ON THE LEAGUE. BUT WHO AND WHY?
THE KRYPTONITE WAS MOVED TO A LARGER RING FOR DESPERO, BUT... THE STONE... THERE'S SOMETHING ABOUT IT...
I SEE IT TOO, CYBORG. IT'S MICRO-SCOPIC.
SOMEONE CARVED OUT A TINY SLIVER FROM THE KRYPTONITE.

DAWN.
THE MAZE OF LEAD PIPES IN THE WALLS AREN'T FUNCTIONAL, ARE THEY?
NO.
AND I ASSUME THE FILE CABINETS ARE TO KEEP VIC OUT?
YES.
SO WHAT IS THIS, BRUCE? YOUR BATCAVE'S BATCAVE?
IT'S A PLACE I HONESTLY DON'T LIKE TO COME TO, CLARK.
WHEN I GAVE YOU THE KRYPTONITE RING, I DID IT UNDER THE PRETENSE THAT UNDER POSSESSION OR MIND CONTROL I COULD PUT EVERYONE AT RISK.
BUT I DIDN'T GIVE YOU THE RING TO INSPIRE ALL OF THIS.
YOU HAVE A BOX FOR EVERY MEMBER OF THE LEAGUE?
YOU WANT ME TO TELL YOU WHY I'M SO CONCERNED ABOUT YOUR RELATIONSHIP WITH WONDER WOMAN?
I THOUGHT YOU ALREADY DID.
OPEN IT.
CHAK

IT'S *EMPTY.*
BECAUSE WONDER WOMAN DOESN'T HAVE A *KRYPTONITE,* CLARK.
THE HARD TRUTH IS THAT IF SHE EVER CROSSES THE LINE, *YOU'RE* THE ONLY ONE WHO COULD STOP HER.
YOU'RE THE BOX.
AND I'M COUNTING ON YOU *TOO,* CLARK. IF *I* EVER GET OUT OF CONTROL--
--IF I EVER *CROSS* THAT LINE--
--I HOPE *YOU'RE* THE ONE WHO'S THERE TO STOP *ME.*
HOW CAN YOU *THINK* THIS WAY, BRUCE? ALWAYS PREPARING FOR THE WORST?
IT'S MORE PRAGMATIC THAN HOPING FOR THE BEST.
I COULD *NEVER* PREPARE TO TAKE DOWN MY FRIENDS LIKE THIS.
I KNOW.

THAT'S WHY I MADE THIS.
YOU CAN'T BE SERIOUS.
BRUCE...
TAKE IT, CLARK.
AND IF YOU EVER NEED TO--IF YOU'RE TRULY MY FRIEND--YOU'LL USE IT.
CHAK
"THIS IS MESSED UP."

I CAN'T DO IT ANYMORE.
YOU DON'T HAVE A CHOICE, RHONDA.
NO.
NO, I JUST CAN'T.
HOW MUCH LONGER COULD I?
I'LL GIVE UP THE SIZE-CHANGING BELT. YOU CAN FIND SOMEONE ELSE.
THE JUSTICE LEAGUE ARE REALLY, REALLY NICE PEOPLE.
THEY'RE THE GOOD GUYS!
AND NOW EVERYONE IS ASKING ME HOW I STOPPED DESPERO! BATMAN WANTS ME TO WALK THEM THROUGH IT. WHAT AM I SUPPOSED TO SAY?! THEY'RE GOING TO FIND OUT!
YOU NEED TO TAKE A BREATH, CALM DOWN AND COME TALK TO US FACE-TO-FACE, RHONDA.
SECRETS.
WE ALL HAVE THEM.

THIS IS ONE OF MINE.
HELLO, AGENT PINEDA.
DIRECTOR WALLER. COLONEL TREVOR. YOU NEED TO LET ME QUIT.
THERE'S SOMETHING REALLY WEIRD GOING ON WITH THE JUSTICE LEAGUE.
TREVOR

SOMEONE HACKED INTO THE WATCHTOWER AND STOLE THEIR FILES.
THEN SOMEONE TOOK SOME KRYPTONITE FROM BATMAN AND GAVE IT TO DESPERO.
AND AFTER WE RECOVERED IT, WE FOUND A SLIVER MISSING.

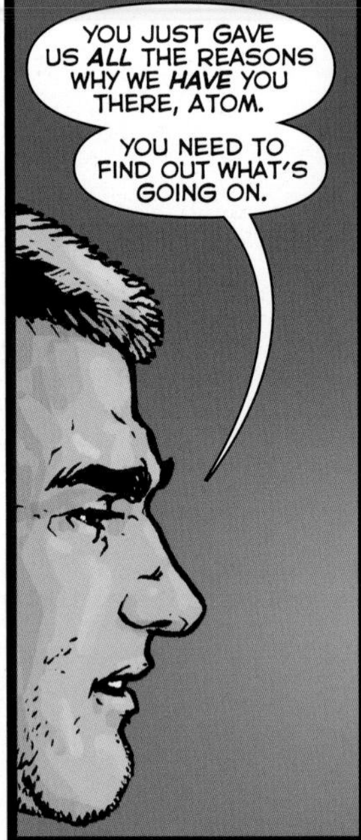
YOU JUST GAVE US ALL THE REASONS WHY WE HAVE YOU THERE, ATOM.
YOU NEED TO FIND OUT WHAT'S GOING ON.

I FEEL LIKE SUCH A BAD PERSON.
YOU'RE NOT.
TREVOR

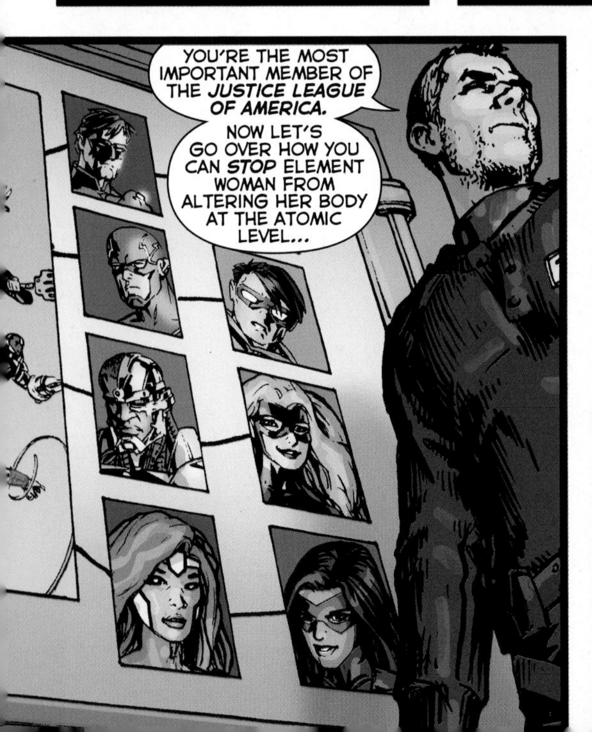
YOU'RE THE MOST IMPORTANT MEMBER OF THE JUSTICE LEAGUE OF AMERICA.
NOW LET'S GO OVER HOW YOU CAN STOP ELEMENT WOMAN FROM ALTERING HER BODY AT THE ATOMIC LEVEL...

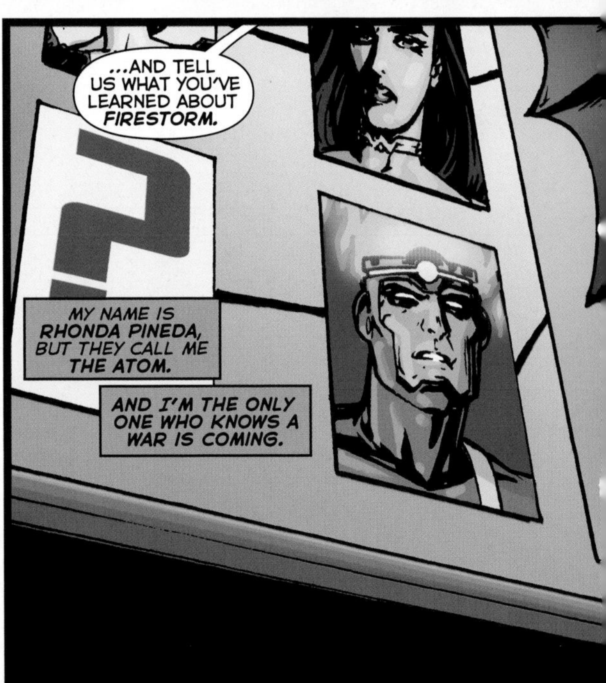
...AND TELL US WHAT YOU'VE LEARNED ABOUT FIRESTORM.
MY NAME IS RHONDA PINEDA, BUT THEY CALL ME THE ATOM.
AND I'M THE ONLY ONE WHO KNOWS A WAR IS COMING.

TRINITY WAR: THE DEATH CARD

GEOFF JOHNS writer **IVAN REIS** penciller **JOE PRADO** and **OCLAIR ALBERT** inkers **ROD REIS** colorist **IVAN REIS, JOE PRADO** and **ROD REIS** cover arists

I HAVEN'T ALWAYS DONE THE RIGHT THING. IN FACT, I SPENT MOST OF MY LIFE DOING EVERYTHING BUT.
YOU SURE THIS IS THE PLACE?
YOU WANTED CHRYSTIE STREET, DIDN'T YOU?
YES, BUT--
THIS IS THE ONLY CHRYSTIE STREET NEAR GREENWICH VILLAGE, HON.
I BELIEVED MYSELF WICKED AT HEART AND USED MY POWER IN INIQUITOUS WAYS.
I WAS LOST.
WAIT!
IT'S NOT HERE!
CAFE
THEN I MET A MAGICIAN NAMED JOHN ZATARA. JOHN TAUGHT ME THAT IT WAS NEVER TOO LATE TO CHOOSE A LIFE OF RECTITUDE.
HE ALSO TAUGHT ME HOW TO HIDE IN PLAIN SIGHT.
PSYCHIC READER
OH.
TAROT READINGS!
PAST PRESENT FUTURE
LIFE ADVISOR
I SIT IN THIS SHOP WAITING FOR THOSE IN DISTRESS TO FIND THEIR WAY TO ME.
I SEE THE TRAGEDY IN THEIR FUTURES.
PAST, PRESENT FUTURE
AND JUST AS JOHN DID WITH ME, I HELP THEM ONTO A DIFFERENT PATH.
PAST, PRESENT
KZZT
FUTURE
I SENSE THIS WOMAN'S DESPERATION, THOUGH FOR SOME REASON LITTLE ELSE.
BUT IF I'M ABLE, I WILL HELP HER.
H-HELLO?
ARE YOU OPEN?
I'M ALWAYS OPEN.

I AM MADAME XANADU.
I SENSE YOU ARE AS MUCH A MYSTERY TO YOURSELF AS YOU ARE TO ME.
MY FRIEND SAID YOU COULD HELP ME.
I'VE BEEN HAVING THIS DREAM--THIS NIGHTMARE--EVERY NIGHT FOR THE LAST WEEK.
I WAKE UP IN MY BED TO THIS SMELL. THERE'S SOMEONE POURING GASOLINE ALL OVER ME. IT'S TOO DARK TO SEE WHO.
THEY THROW A LIT MATCH AND WATCH ME BURN. WHEN THE FIRE LIGHTS UP THE ROOM, I SEE THEM.
AND IT'S ME.
I...I THINK THERE'S SOMETHING EVIL INSIDE OF ME. I THINK IT'S GOING TO MAKE ME DO TERRIBLE THINGS.
TWO NIGHTS AGO, I WOKE UP AND FOUND A CAN OF GASOLINE NEXT TO MY BED. MY FEET WERE DIRTY. I THINK I WAS SLEEPWALKING. I HAVEN'T SLEPT S-SINCE...
I TOUCH HER...
...AND I SEE THE FUTURE.

BUT IT'S NOT HERS.
THERE'S NOTHING LEFT TO FIGHT FOR.
YES, THERE IS.
WE HAVE TO ESCAPE. WE HAVE TO SAVE HIM.
I SEE THE AFTERMATH OF A GREAT WAR. AND I SEE ONE WORD THAT DEFINES IT: TRINITY.
WHAT'S WRONG WITH ME?
WHAT IS THE TRINITY WAR?
THE CARDS.
KZZT
THE CARDS WILL TELL ME WHO WILL START IT AND HOW I CAN STOP THEM.
I HAVE YET TO MEET HIM, BUT I KNOW WHO HE IS.
AND HOW WRONGLY HE WAS CHOSEN.
FWAP
THE BOY

"BLACK ADAM WAS A BAD GUY, BILLY."
I STILL HAVE TO DO SOMETHING WITH HIS ASHES, FREDDY.
THIS HOUSE HAS TWO BATHROOMS.
WHICH IS ENTIRELY TOO FEW FOR SIX KIDS AND TWO ADULTS.
THREE ADULTS IF YOU COUNT BILLY, EUGENE.
YOU MEAN SHAZAM!
NOT SO LOUD, DARLA. MR. AND MRS. VASQUEZ ARE HOME.
BLACK ADAM TRIED TO KILL US. WHY WOULD YOU DO ANYTHING FOR HIM?
BECAUSE HE DIDN'T GO OFF THE DEEP END UNTIL MAGIC CAME INTO THE PICTURE.
YOU'RE NOT GOING TO TURN EVIL LIKE HIM, ARE YOU?
NO, DARLA. AND HE WASN'T EVIL. HE WAS MISGUIDED.
WHERE ARE YOU TAKING HIM?
I'LL SPREAD HIS ASHES ACROSS THE KAHNDAQ DESERT.
KAHNDAQ?
THAT'S WHERE HE WAS FROM, MARY.
THAT'S HALFWAY ACROSS THE WORLD.
BILLY CAN FLY THERE.
IT'S DANGEROUS.
MARY'S RIGHT, BILLY. THE GOVERNMENT HAS ISSUED A STRICT WARNING AGAINST ANY AMERICAN TRAVELING THERE.
SUPERMAN AND WONDER WOMAN WENT THERE TO RESCUE THOSE HOSTAGES LAST WEEK.
BUT WHY DO THIS, BILLY?
BECAUSE EVEN "BAD GUYS" DESERVE TO BE BURIED.

"SHAZAM!"
KRAKOOOM
ADVISOR
WHAT'S GOING TO HAPPEN TO ME?!
THIS ISN'T ABOUT THE POOR GIRL.
THE HERO
THE WARRIOR
IT'S ABOUT THE JUSTICE LEAGUE.
BELLE REVE PRISON.
I CHANGED OUR TICKETS FOR THE LATER SHOW IF YOU'RE STILL UP FOR IT.
I'D LIKE THAT, BUT I DON'T HAVE FAITH DESPERO'S GOING TO STAY HERE FOR LONG, LET ALONE THE NIGHT.
WHEN HAL SHOWS UP ON EARTH AGAIN, WE'LL ASK HIM TO TRANSFER DESPERO TO OA.
BUT HE'LL EVENTUALLY ESCAPE.
THERE'S A REASON I DON'T HAVE A LIST OF VILLAINS AS LONG AS BRUCE'S, BARRY'S OR EVEN YOURS.
WHEN I DEAL WITH THEM, I DEAL WITH THEM.

I TRUST YOU'RE NOT TALKING ABOUT KILLING THEM, DIANA.
ONLY IF IT COMES TO THAT.
THERE'S NO DOUBT INNOCENT PEOPLE HAVE BEEN PUT ON DEATH ROW.
NOT IF YOU HAVE A LASSO OF TRUTH.
MAYBE WE SHOULD CHANGE THE SUBJECT.
NO.
FWAP
"NOT HER."
SUPERMAN.

YOU'RE THE PUREST OF HEART. YOU HAVE TO BE.
MOST WOULD ARGUE OTHERWISE, BUT I BELIEVE PANDORA IS THE WORST OF THEM. SO DID JOHN.
THE HOSTAGE
PANDORA IS ONE OF THE SCORNED TRINITY OF SIN.
THREE TRANSGRESSORS WHO WERE DAMNED BY AN ANCIENT COUNCIL TO AN ETERNAL LIFE, WALKING AMONG US AND WITNESSING WHAT THEY HAD WROUGHT.
PANDORA?
PANDORA? AS IN THE GREEK MYTH?
YOU'RE IN A RELATIONSHIP WITH ONE OF THOSE MYTHS, SUPERMAN. WE'RE VERY REAL.
IF THE GODS SENT YOU--
LIKE YOU, I NEVER LISTEN TO THE GODS, DIANA.
I BELIEVE ONE OF THEM GOT ME INTO THIS MESS IN THE FIRST PLACE.
SOMEONE MANIPULATED ME INTO OPENING THIS BOX, DAMNING MYSELF--AND ALL OF HUMANITY.
I FREED THE SEVEN SINS FROM THEIR PRISON.
"BECAUSE OF ME, HUMANS HAVE THE CAPACITY FOR EVIL.
"BUT WITH YOUR HELP, I CAN FOREVER ERADICATE EVIL."
YOU WANT TO RECRUIT DOCTOR LIGHT, AMANDA?
I SEE A SECOND JUSTICE LEAGUE NOW...A TEAM BUILT BY DESIGN INSTEAD OF FATE.

WASHINGTON, D.C.
THE HEADQUARTERS OF THE JUSTICE LEAGUE OF AMERICA.
PUT TOGETHER TO SPECIFICALLY COUNTER THE JUSTICE LEAGUE IN EVERY WAY...WITHOUT MOST OF THEIR RECRUITS EVEN REALIZING IT.
IF I JOIN THE JLA, THEY'LL HELP ME FIND A CURE TO THESE POWERS.
BECAUSE THESE ABILITIES HAVE DONE SOMETHING TO ME, KIM.
EVERY ROOM I WALK INTO, I TAKE AWAY THE LIGHT. I SUCK IT UP LIKE A BLACK HOLE.
I CRAVE DARKNESS.
AND NOW THEY WANT ME TO USE THIS POWER AGAINST FIRESTORM.
BUT HE'S ACTUALLY TWO KIDS.
AND THE LAST THING I WANT TO DO IS HURT KIDS.
"YOU SAID YOU COULD TRUST DOCTOR LIGHT, AMANDA, BUT HE'S ALREADY TOLD HIS WIFE EVERYTHING."

YOU DO REALIZE ARTHUR LIGHT IS A SCIENTIST, NOT A SOLDIER, DON'T YOU?
THAT'S EXACTLY WHY WE NEED HIM, STEVE.
LIGHT LITERALLY WROTE THE BOOK ON METAHUMAN PHYSICS AND POWER GENERATION--HE KNOWS HOW FIRESTORM'S ABILITIES WORK BETTER THAN FIRESTORM DOES.
INCLUDING THE TRUTH BEHIND THIS COUNTRY'S SHINY NEW HOPE--THE JUSTICE LEAGUE OF AMERICA. SHE KNOWS IT'S A FRONT--
WE'LL SEND THE MARTIAN TO PAY MRS. LIGHT A VISIT TO TAKE THAT INFORMATION BACK.
AND I'LL WARN ARTHUR THAT IF HE TALKS TO HIS WIFE AGAIN, WE'LL ERASE HIM FROM HER MIND.
THE BOY
FWAP
FWAP
THE POLITICIAN
THE SOLDIER
DO WE HAVE AN UNDER-STANDING?
YES, DIRECTOR WALLER.

FWP
THE DETECTI
HAPPY HARBOR, RHODE ISLAND.
THE REMAINS OF THE JUSTICE LEAGUE WATCHTOWER.
SOMEONE HACKS INTO OUR SYSTEM WITHOUT MY KNOWING, SHUTS DOWN OUR DEFENSES AND LETS DESPERO IN.
WHILE SOMEONE ELSE--OR MAYBE THE SAME PERSON--BREAKS INTO THE BATCAVE AND STEALS A KRYPTONITE RING.
A KRYPTONITE RING NO ONE KNEW YOU HAD.
I HAVE IT FOR STUDY, VIC.
TO SEE IF YOU CAN COME UP WITH A KRYPTONITE ANTIDOTE FOR SUPERMAN?
THAT MIGHT FLY WITH THE ROOKIES, BRUCE, BUT NOT WITH ME.
BATMAN SAID TO KEEP OUR EYES OPEN FOR ANYTHING SALVAGEABLE FROM THE TROPHY ROOM, ELEMENT WOMAN.
I CAN'T BELIEVE YOU STOPPED DESPERO ALL BY YOURSELF, ATOM.
THAT IS THE COOLEST THING THAT'S EVER HAPPENED IN THE HISTORY OF HAPPENINGS.
YEAH, UH, BEGINNER'S LUCK.
TELL NO ONE I WAS HERE.
HEY! I THINK I FOUND SOME-THING!
IT'S A CHESS SET...

"...BUT THE SUPERMAN PIECE IS MISSING."
HUMANS AREN'T EVIL BECAUSE SOMEONE OPENED A MAGIC BOX, PANDORA. WHOEVER TOLD YOU THAT--
NO ONE TOLD ME ANYTHING. I WAS THERE. I SAW THE SEVEN SINS FLY OUT INTO THE WORLD.
I CAN'T HAVE THIS CONVERSATION. DIANA?
THAT'S WHAT HAPPENED, SUPERMAN. SOMEONE TRICKED HER INTO OPENING THE BOX.
BUT THERE'S SOMEONE OUT THERE WHO CAN UNDO WHAT I DID. SOMEONE WHO CAN OPEN THIS BOX AND IMPRISON SIN ONCE AGAIN.
WE CAN FREE HUMANITY FROM EVIL. AND I CAN BE FREE FROM MY CURSE.
YOU JUST NEED TO OPEN THE BOX. AND IF ANYONE CAN SURVIVE ITS TOUCH, IT'S SUPERMAN!
AHH!
SUPERMAN?!

AAHHHH!

WHAT DID YOU DO?
THE BOX...
WHAT'S IT DOING TO HIM?
HE SHOULD HAVE BEEN ABLE TO OVERCOME THE INFLUENCE. HE'S SUPERMAN.
THERE'S NO EVIL IN SUPERMAN!
GET THE BOX AWAY FROM HIM, PANDORA.
NOW!
CHAK
CHAK
HE'S MORE HUMAN THAN I REALIZED.

BLAMM
BLAMM
STOP!
KA-TANG
PANDORA?
SUPERMAN? WONDER WOMAN? WE'VE GOT AN EMERGENCY.
SO DO WE, BATMAN. SUPERMAN'S--
NO. I'M OKAY, DIANA... AND PANDORA'S GONE.
WE'LL EXPLAIN LATER. WHAT'S THE EMERGENCY, BATMAN?
CYBORG JUST GOT A VISUAL ON SOMEONE IN A CAPE FLYING INTO KAHNDAQ.
WHO IS IT?
A NEW SUPER-HUMAN FROM PHILADELPHIA--SHAZAM. HE'S CROSSED THE BORDER, BUT HE DOESN'T SEEM TO REALIZE THE KAHNDAQI ARMY IS ON HIS TAIL.
"WHEN YOU TWO WENT INTO KAHNDAQ YOURSELVES, IT MADE IT OKAY FOR EVERYONE ELSE."
"WHAT DO WE KNOW ABOUT SHAZAM?"
"FROM THE ENERGY SIGNATURE CYBORG'S DETECTED, WE SUSPECT SHAZAM'S POWERED BY MAGIC--SOMETHING WE DON'T HAVE A LOT OF EXPERIENCE WITH."
"ZATANNA SAID IF WE EVER NEEDED HER, SHE'D BE THERE FOR US."

"WE'RE ALREADY MAKING A CALL."
YES! WE'RE HEADING INTO KAHNDAQ RIGHT NOW, COLONEL TREVOR.
DOCTOR LIGHT.
GET YOUR HELMET STRAPPED ON AND GET TO THE INVISIBLE JET.
"THE JUSTICE LEAGUE IS HEADING INTO KAHNDAQ.
"IT'S THE JLA'S JOB TO GET THEM OUT."
THE JLA ISN'T READY FOR THIS, WALLER.
THIS IS AN OPPORTUNITY WE MIGHT NOT GET AGAIN, STEVE.
THIS IS OUR CHANCE TO GO SHINE A SPOT-LIGHT ON HOW UNCONTROLLABLE THE JUSTICE LEAGUE IS.
THEY WANT US TO FORCE THE JUSTICE LEAGUE TO DO SOMETHING? THIS IS CRAZY, STARGIRL.
I'M SUPPOSED TO TAKE ON THE FLASH?
WHAT CAN I DO AGAINST CYBORG?
YOU GOT AQUAMAN? YOU DON'T, UH, YOU DON'T WANT TO TRADE DO YOU, HAWKMAN?
NO, VIBE.
BUT I'LL TAKE YOURS TOO IF YOU DON'T THINK YOU CAN HANDLE IT.
WHATEVER THEY'RE DOING, IF BATMAN'S INVOLVED, WE SHOULD TRUST THEM.
YOUR PERSONAL INVESTMENT IS CLOUD-ING YOUR JUDGMENT, CATWOMAN.
WHY'S IT GETTING DARK IN HERE?
THIS IS WRONG.

THE JUSTICE LEAGUE HAS SAVED THE WORLD COUNTLESS TIMES.
THE JLA SHOULD BE THERE TO SUPPORT THEM.
THE NEW GUY IS RIGHT, COLONEL TREVOR.
IF THEY'RE GOING INTO KAHNDAQ, THEY'VE GOT A GOOD REASON TO.
GOOD REASON OR NOT, THIS CALLS FOR DIPLOMACY BEFORE ACTION, LANTERN.
WHICH IS EXACTLY WHAT WE'RE NOT DOING.
I'M NO FAN OF THE LEAGUE, TREVOR, BUT THEY AREN'T THE BAD GUYS.
WE'RE UNDER DIRECT ORDERS, ARROW. YOU DON'T LIKE IT, GET OFF THE JET.
THIS ISN'T HOW I PLANNED ON THIS GOING DOWN.
NOR I.
BUT YOU'RE WRONG, STEVE. AFTER EVERYTHING THAT HAPPENED WITH THE SECRET SOCIETY...
...WE ARE READY TO TAKE ON THE JUSTICE LEAGUE.
TRUE INTENTIONS ARE HIDDEN BY LIES.
THE ALIEN
THE MARTIAN MANHUNTER ISN'T THE ONLY ONE MASQUERAD-ING AMONG THEM.

THEY ALL HAVE SECRETS.
I GUESS I SHOULD SAY SOMETHING.
I'VE NEVER BEEN ANY GOOD AT THIS.
HEY!
BRRAATTT
DON'T--!
KSHH
NO!
I FLEW ALL THE WAY HERE AND... AND YOU RUINED IT.
STOP SHOOTING AT ME!

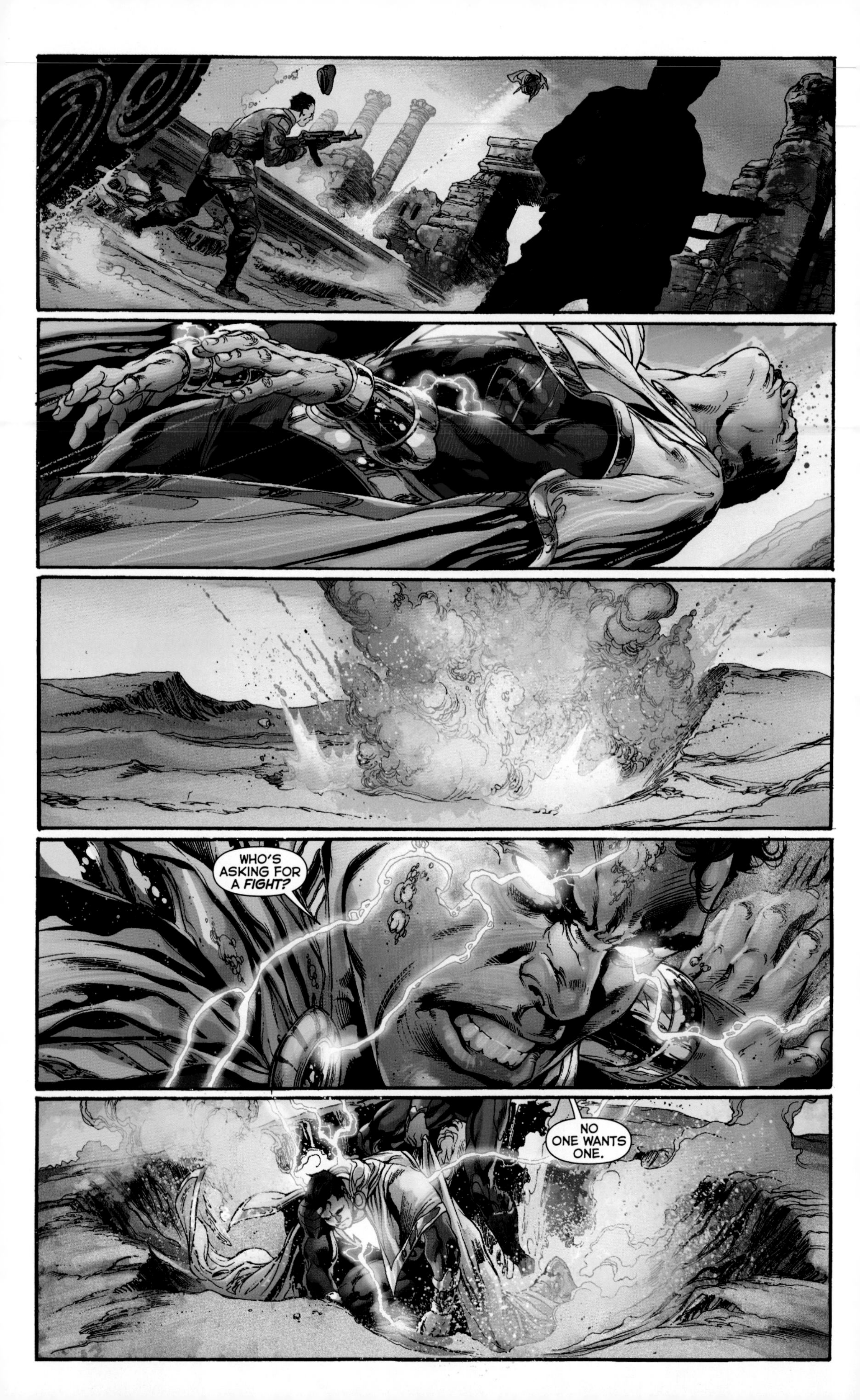
WHO'S ASKING FOR A FIGHT?
NO ONE WANTS ONE.

THEN YOU SHOULDN'T HAVE *STARTED* IT!
SUPERMAN?
I JUST KNOCKED DOWN SUPERMAN.
I JUST KNOCKED DOWN SUPERMAN.

WHAT ARE YOU DOING IN KAHNDAQ?
OR *WHAT?*
I'D ANSWER THE LADY.
YOU AREN'T SO TOUGH, SUPERMAN!
YOU HAVEN'T *SEEN* ME BE YET.

I ASK AGAIN--WHAT ARE YOU DOING IN KAHNDAQ?
WHAT BUSINESS IS IT OF YOURS, HUH?
JERKS.
WELL, HE'S A BIT RUDE, ISN'T HE?
WHO IS HE?
THERE'S SOMETHING FAMILIAR ABOUT SHAZAM'S MAGIC. LIKE I'VE BEEN IN ITS PRESENCE BEFORE.
WHATEVER YOU AND THE REST OF THE LEAGUE ARE DOING HERE, ZATANNA...

...WE'RE GOING TO ESCORT YOU *OUT.*

THAT'S WHAT WE CAME TO DO WITH SHAZAM, STEVE.
KAHNDAQ THINKS THEY'RE BEING INVADED, DIANA.
COME WITH US BEFORE THIS ESCALATES.
THOSE SOLDIERS WERE THE ONES THAT JUST STARTED FIRING.
THEN SUPERMAN HIT ME.
WHAT WAS I SUPPOSED TO DO?
TELL DIRECTOR WALLER AND HER GOVERNMENT WATCHDOGS, THE JUSTICE LEAGUE HAS THIS UNDER CONTROL. TAKE YOUR "TEAM" BACK TO D.C.
AND THIS IS NO PLACE FOR YOU, CATWOMAN.
IT'S NOT EXACTLY YOUR SCENE EITHER, BATMAN. THOUGHT TRUTHFULLY, I'VE ALWAYS THOUGHT YOU COULD USE A LITTLE MORE SUN.
WE'VE GOT THE KAHNDAQ AIR FORCE FLYING OVERHEAD. THIS ISN'T A JOKE, CATWOMAN.
OF COURSE IT IS, STEVIE. NOW COME ON. DON'T YOU WANT TO MAKE WONDER GIRL AND BATS A LITTLE JEALOUS?
I SEE YET ANOTHER PLAYER IN THIS GAME.
ANOTHER MYSTERY.
FWAP
UNKNOWN

WILL YOU STOP TURNING OVER CARDS AND PLEASE TELL ME WHAT YOU SEE?
EVIL
OH, I MESSED UP. I NEVER SHOULD'VE AGREED TO BEING PART OF THE JLA.
I NEVER SHOULD'VE DONE THIS.
"DONE WHAT, ATOM?"
EVIL
PANDORA IS FINALLY OUT IN THE OPEN.
"SHE WILL SOON BELONG TO THE SOCIETY."
I NEED TO FIND SOMEONE ELSE TO HELP ME.
I MUST OPEN THIS BOX.
IT'S TIME THE PHANTOM STRANGER GOT INVOLVED.
WHAT IS THE QUESTION I MUST ANSWER NEXT?

WHO IS THE EVIL BEHIND THE EVIL?
WHO IS THE EVIL BEHIND THE EVIL
EVIL
EVIL
DARKSEID INVADES
SUPER VILLAINS
HAVE A NICE DAY
EVIL
STRANGE LIGHTS ABOVE THE KIELDER FOREST

WE ALL NEED TO STOP!
PLEASE!
STAND YOUR GROUND, DOCTOR LIGHT.
NO!
MY WIFE'S ALWAYS SAID AS LONG AS WE WANT THE SAME THING, WE CAN FIGURE THINGS OUT. AND WE ALL DO WANT THE SAME THING, DON'T WE?
WE ALL JUST WANT TO DO WHAT'S RIGHT.
AAAH!
DOCTOR LIGHT?!
SUPERMAN... HE'S A SOLAR BATTERY. I C-CAN'T--
AAHH!
DIANA!
GET AWAY FROM HER!
SUPERMAN, I'M SORRY! I--!

NO!
I KNOW WHAT THE TRINITY MEANS.
THEY'RE COMING. SOME OF THEM ARE ALREADY HERE.
I NEED TO WARN THE JUSTICE LEAGUES!
N-NO... I DIDN'T MEAN TO...
DOCTOR LIGHT?
SUPERMAN KILLED HIM.
SUPERMAN DID NOT DO THIS!
WHAT HAVE I DONE?
WHO IS TRYING TO IMPUTE THE MAN OF STEEL?
MY FRIENDS TOLD THE TRUTH ABOUT YOU.
YOU REALLY DO SEE THE FUTURE.
AAHHH!
BUT THE SECRET SOCIETY MADE SURE YOU WOULDN'T SEE ME COMING.
WHO ARE YOU?
THEY CALL ME PLASTIQUE.
AND YOU WON'T WARN ANYONE ABOUT THE FUTURE EVER AGAIN.
AU REVOIR, MADEMOISELLE.

STOP!
PLEASE STOP!

THE HOSTAGE
THE BETRAYER
PLEASE!

THE GAMEPLAYER
THE GRID
THE ARCHER
THE THIEF

THE FREA
THE MESSENGER
THE KING
THE MAGICIAN
THE SPIRIT
THE MIRACLE WORKER
THE MISFIT
THE SAVAG
THE ASSASSIN

...REPORTS COMING IN OF AN ALL-OUT WAR BETWEEN THE JUSTICE LEAGUE AND THE JUSTICE LEAGUE OF AMERICA.
THE DETECTIVE
THE HERO
THE SACRIFICE
THE WARRIOR
...ONE CASUALTY, THOUGH I'M NOT SURE I BELIEVE IT...AT THE HANDS OF SUPERMAN?
THIS CAN'T BE TRUE.
HA.
THANKS TO ME, EVERYONE WILL ACTUALLY BELIEVE THAT SUPERMAN'S KILLED DOCTOR LIGHT.
THE OUTSIDER
"AND BY THE TIME THE JUSTICE LEAGUE FIGURES OUT WHAT I'M UP TO, THE WORLD WILL ALREADY BELONG TO US."

TRINITY WAR: CONCLUSION

GEOFF JOHNS writer **IVAN REIS** penciller **JOE PRADO, OCLAIR ALBERT** and **EBER FERREIRA** inkers
ROD REIS colorist **DOUG MAHNKE** and **ALEX SINCLAIR** cover artists

IT ALL STARTED FIVE YEARS AGO.
THE PLANET WAS ATTACKED BY ONE OF THE MOST POWERFUL BEINGS IN EXISTENCE -- A WORLD CONQUEROR CALLED
DARKSEID.
THE JUSTICE LEAGUE CAME TOGETHER TO STOP HIM FROM ENSLAVING EARTH.

ON THAT SAME DAY, WHILE THE BARRIERS BETWEEN UNIVERSES WERE WEAKENED, I FINALLY ESCAPED FROM WHAT WAS LEFT OF MY WORLD.
BUT MY MASTER DID NOT.
THEY DIDN'T MAKE IT.
NO, MY DEAR, BUT WE DID.
HA.
AND SO MY MISSION TO SAVE HIM BEGAN.
THE JUSTICE LEAGUE CONTINUED TO BATTLE OVERT THREATS TO THE WORLD WHILE WE STAYED HIDDEN.
WHEN I DISCOVERED THE EXISTENCE OF PANDORA'S BOX I FELT HOPE.
I RECOGNIZED IT.
I KNEW WHERE IT CAME FROM AND WHAT IT COULD DO.
I RECRUITED THE LEAGUE'S MANY ENEMIES, STARTING WITH PROFESSOR IVO.

FOR THE FIRST YEAR, I STRUGGLED TO COMPREHEND THE CULTURE AND RULES OF THIS BIZARRE PLACE.
EVEN THE VERY BASIC OF IDEAS APPEARED TWISTED AND TURNED INSIDE OUT.
EAST IS WEST AND WEST IS EAST.
WHILE THE LEAGUE CONTINUED ON, I SEARCHED FOR A WAY TO HELP THE MAN WHO RESCUED ME FROM MY DESTITUTE LIFE.
I HAD MANY MOMENTS OF DOUBT AND DESPERATION DURING THIS TIME.
I FELT ALONE.
BUT I REFUSED TO FAIL MY MASTER.
I BEGAN BUILDING THE SECRET SOCIETY TO BE AT THE READY FOR MY MASTER'S ARRIVAL.
THEN I PLANTED AN AGENT WITHIN THE JUSTICE LEAGUE'S RANKS.
AND WITH THE HIGH LEVEL OF DISTRUST BETWEEN THE LEAGUES, I KNEW IT WAS ONLY A MATTER OF TIME BEFORE OPPORTUNITY WOULD PRESENT ITSELF.
WHEN THE LEAGUES CAME INTO CONFLICT, I MADE THE WORLD BELIEVE SUPERMAN HAD KILLED ONE OF HIS WOULD-BE TEAMMATES. THEY THOUGHT IT TO BE BECAUSE OF HIS ENCOUNTER WITH PANDORA'S BOX.
SO THE LEAGUES SET OFF TO FIND IT. THEY'VE DONE MY JOB FOR ME.
HA.
I AM AN OUTSIDER TO THIS WORLD.
I AM THE OUTSIDER.
AND I SERVE MY MASTER WELL.

I'VE TRACKED BATMAN'S SIGNAL HERE.
WHERE IS HERE, CYBORG?
THE TEMPLE OF HEPHAESTUS IN ATHENS.
THERE ARE OTHERS ALREADY INSIDE, BUT MY TELEPATHY IS AGAIN BEING BLOCKED.
THE SOCIETY MUST BE HERE TOO.
OR AT LEAST, ITS LEADER.
ALTHOUGH MY WORLD IS FOREVER LOST...THIS ONE CAN BE OURS.
THE BOX ISN'T A PRISON, BATMAN, IT'S A DOORWAY.
A DOORWAY TO WHERE, MADAME XANADU?
YOU NEED TO GO AWAY, BATS. GET EVERYONE OUTTA HERE RIGHT NOW.
SO WE CAN LEAVE THE BOX IN YOUR HANDS, CONSTANTINE?

THIS ONE WILL BE OURS.
THEY BROUGHT THE BOX HERE, WONDER WOMAN. BACK TO WHERE I FIRST FOUND IT.
YOU NEED TO LET ME HELP--
YOU'VE HELPED ENOUGH, PANDORA.
WHAT'S WRONG, VIBE?
I'VE GOT ONE OF MY, UH, "VIBE" HEADACHES, FLASH...
...THERE'S SOMETHING THAT'S NOT FROM OUR UNIVERSE NEARBY. OR SOMEONE. MAYBE BOTH.
THE BLOODY THING CORRUPTS WHOEVER TOUCHES IT. 'CEPT FOR ME, RIGHT? I'M ALREADY GOOD AN' GONE.
BUT YOU CAPES DON'T KNOW HOW TA DEAL WITH THAT DARK VOICE CREEPING IN YOUR HEADS. IT'S ALREADY GOT SHAZAM!
TELL 'EM, LUV. ZATANNA?
ZEE?
IF MY FATHER WERE ALIVE, HE'D HAVE KILLED YOU FOR THE WAY YOU TREATED ME.
BLIMEY.
NOT YOU TOO.

NOT *EVERYONE*.

EVIG EM EHT XOB!

I CAN'T BE THE ONLY ONE WITH MY HEAD SCREWED ON STRAIGHT. DON'T YOU BLOODY SEE?
WHATEVER EVIL IS INSIDE THE BOX IS LEAKIN' OUT. IT'S ALREADY INFECTING Y--
SHUT UP, OLD MAN.
--AAAARGHHH!!
HA.
IT'S TIME.

BATMAN'S GOT THE BOX! WE CAN HELP SUPERMAN--
YOU THINK I CARE ABOUT WHAT HAPPENS TO SUPERMAN, LANTERN?
HE TOOK DIANA FROM ME, SIMON. LET HIM ROT.
YOU'RE JUST A MAN.
I'M NOT AFRAID OF YOU, BATMAN. I'M THE GREEN LANTERN.
BUT YOU'RE NO HAL JORDAN.
HEY, NEW GUY.

YOU SHOULD WORRY ABOUT ME.

I'VE GOT MUSCLES, FRANKIE.
N-NO, YOU D-DON'T.
SHAZAM!
KRAKKKOOOMMMM
MERA?
WHAT ARE YOU DOING HERE?
SHE'S NOT.
BLAMM
WHAT HAPPENS IF I OPEN THE BOX? WOULD I EARN FORGIVENESS IN THE EYES OF THE GODS?
WOULD I FINALLY GET THE ANSWER TO: WHO AM I?
I CANNOT ALLOW THAT TO HAPPEN, QUESTION!
YOU'LL BECOME MORE DANGEROUS THAN THE BOX ITSELF!

GIVE IT TO ME, BATMAN. I CAN DESTROY IT.
WHICH WOULD OPEN IT, DIANA. AND THAT'S THE LAST THING I THINK WE SHOULD BE DOING.
WE NEED TO SAVE SUPERMAN.
I'M HERE, DIANA.
BUT YOU'RE SICK. AND I'M WORRIED YOU'LL DIE IF BATMAN DOESN'T HAND IT OVER.
WHAT?
AND AFTER I DIE WHAT WILL YOU DO? WILL YOU GO BACK TO STEVE?
OR WILL YOU GO TO BATMAN?
THIS IS ALL GOING BAD, TREVOR. WE'VE GOT WAVES OF EVIL THOUGHTS HITTING EVERYONE.
I HOPE SUPERMAN DIES.
THE BOX IS AFFECTING US. WE NEED TO--
DON'T TELL ME WHAT I NEED TO DO, BATMAN. I WANT TO LIVE A FULL LIFE AND THAT INCLUDES SHARING IT.
AND I WON'T LET YOU TAKE HER AWAY FROM ME.
SUPERMAN, STOP!

I WON'T STOP UNTIL BATMAN IS DEAD!

BOOOOOMMMM
KZZZT
THOOOMM
SUPERMAN?!
NOBODY TOUCH THE BOX!
IT'S GONE DORMANT FOR THE MOMENT.
EVERYBODY STAY BACK.
WHY IS THE BOX HURTING SUPERMAN PHYSICALLY, BUT NOT US?
WONDER WOMAN?

THE BOX MIGHT BE MAKING ALL OF US A LITTLE CRAZY IN THE HEAD, BUT I DON'T THINK IT'S WHAT'S MAKING SUPERMAN SICK.
I DIDN'T SEE IT BEFORE BECAUSE IT'S SO FAINT, BUT...IT'S GETTING STRONGER.
WHAT IS IT, FIRE-STORM?
I SEE IT TOO, RONNIE.
SUPERMAN'S EMITTING SOME KIND OF RADIOACTIVE AURA... IT'S...
WE WOULDN'T HAVE RECOGNIZED IT WITHOUT WALLER'S HELP.
IT'S KRYPTONITE.
HE'S BEING POISONED BY KRYPTONITE? WHERE IS IT?
I THINK IT'S COMING FROM INSIDE SUPERMAN.
I CAN FIND IT.
I CAN TURN INTO OXYGEN AND ENTER HIS BLOOD-STREAM. THEN TRACE THE DYING CELLS BACK TO THE SOURCE.
IT... IT'S IN HIS BRAIN.
HIS BRAIN?
THERE'S A MICROSCOPIC SLIVER OF KRYPTONITE IN THERE.
HOW'D A MICROSCOPIC SLIVER OF KRYPTONITE GET IN HIS BRAIN?
OH, THAT'S AN EASY QUESTION TO ANSWER, CYBORG.

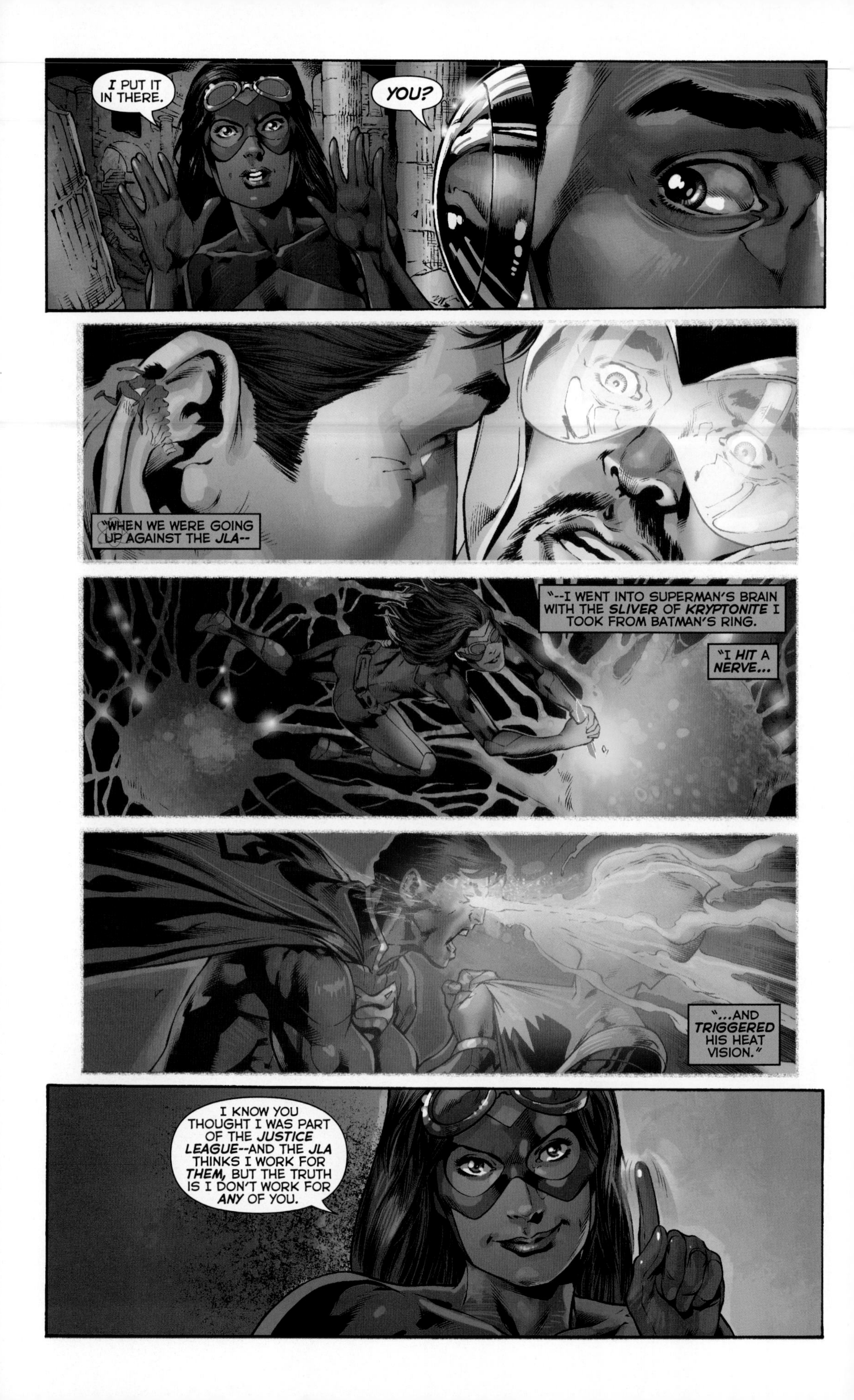
I PUT IT IN THERE.
YOU?
"WHEN WE WERE GOING UP AGAINST THE JLA--
"--I WENT INTO SUPERMAN'S BRAIN WITH THE SLIVER OF KRYPTONITE I TOOK FROM BATMAN'S RING.
"I HIT A NERVE...
"...AND TRIGGERED HIS HEAT VISION."
I KNOW YOU THOUGHT I WAS PART OF THE JUSTICE LEAGUE--AND THE JLA THINKS I WORK FOR THEM, BUT THE TRUTH IS I DON'T WORK FOR ANY OF YOU.

SO YOU'RE A TRAITOR?
OH, VIC.
HONEY.
SO ARE YOU.
VEET
YES.
I HAVE NO NEED FOR THIS FLESH ANYMORE.
N-NO...
AND IT IS A WEAKNESS I PREFER TO BE WITHOUT.
SO I WILL SEPARATE FROM IT.
CHANK
CHANK
CHANK

AARRGHHHHH!

VICTOR!
KRRZZZAATTT
KRRAAZZZAARTTTT
RRRAAAARR!
VIC?!
KW-KW-KW
KLINK

GRID
ON-LINE.

IT'S OURS.
KKKRAKKKZZTTTT
WHOEVER YOU ARE, YOU CAN'T YAAAHH!
IT'S TOO LATE, FLASH.
I DON'T UNDERSTAND.
YOU NEVER DID, PANDORA.
SINCE THE GODS WHO DAMNED YOU FIRST FOUND THIS BOX, THEY BELIEVED IT TO BE MAGIC.
BUT THEY WERE WRONG.
IT'S SCIENCE.

ALL THIS TIME YOU SEARCHED THIS WORLD FOR SOMEONE WHO COULD OPEN THE BOX. BUT ONLY SOMEONE FROM OUR WORLD CAN DO THAT, PANDORA.
HA.
LIKE THE MOTHER BOX, THIS IS ONLY ONE OF MANY. AND LIKE THE MOTHER BOX, "PANDORA'S BOX" CAN OPEN A GATEWAY TO ANOTHER UNIVERE.
OUR UNIVERSE.
THE BIRTHPLACE OF EVIL.

IT WAS CREATED ON MY WORLD LONG AGO. AND LEFT HERE.
ALL THIS TIME YOU WERE LOOKING FOR WHO WAS BEHIND THIS...AS YOU SAY ON YOUR WORLD...
...THE BUTLER DID IT.
WHAT'S HAPPENING, DEADMAN?
HE JUST OPENED SOME KIND OF PORTAL.
SOMEONE'S COMING THROUGH.

BATMAN?
STAY WITH ME, VIC.
WHO IS THAT? WHAT THE HELL IS GOING ON?

THE BOX HAS BEEN DESTROYED.
BUT EVIL HASN'T BEEN IMPRISONED, PANDORA. ONLY UNLEASHED!
THE TRINITY... IT WASN'T ABOUT YOU...
...IT WAS THE NUMBER... THE TRUE NUMBER OF EVIL.
THREE.
EARTH-THREE.
FINALLY!
THOUGH THE SEA KING DIDN'T MAKE IT...

...WE HAVE SURVIVED.

WHO ARE THEY?
I DON'T KNOW, CATWOMAN. EVERYONE REGROUP.
NOW!
JOHNNY?!
ATOMICA!
ATOMICA?
SHE'S ONE OF THEM.
OH, JOHNNY, DID I MISS YOU.
THIS WORLD IS SUCH A DRAG.
WE'LL MAKE IT FUN, BABY. PROMISE.
WELCOME TO YOUR NEW HOME, MASTER THOMAS.
HA.
IT TOOK YOU LONG ENOUGH, ALFRED.
B-BUT IS IT S-SAFE, OWLMAN?
IT DOESN'T LOOK S-SAFE!

IT LOOKS DANGEROUS!
CALM YOURSELF, POWER RING. THIS IS A FASCINATING WORLD, NOT A DANGEROUS ONE. NOT TO US.
B-BUT WHAT IS THAT?!
B-BUT DEATHSTORM--
KEEP PANICKING AND YOU WILL ONLY MAKE YOUR CONDITION WORSE.
THIS IS GRID.
I MET HIM WHEN I WAS HACKING INTO CYBORG.
NICE FIND, BABY.
GRID IS A SENTIENT COMPUTER VIRUS FROM THIS WORLD WITH ASPIRATIONS BEYOND CORRUPTING FILES.
HAVE A NICE DAY.
IF WE HAVE ANYTHING TO WORRY ABOUT, POWER RING, IT'S OUR PRISONER.
WE SHOULD'VE LEFT THE BASTARD ON OUR WORLD.
WE NEED TO REMOVE THE KRYPTONITE FROM SUPERMAN!
WE NEED TO GET VIC STABILIZED.
THE REST OF YOU, THOSE THAT CAN STAND--
IT'S SO DISCONCERTING, ISN'T IT?
YES.
THEY LOOK LIKE US, SUPER-WOMAN.
AND LIKE OUR LOST ALLIES.
THEY'RE TRYING TO GET UP! WHAT DO WE DO, ULTRAMAN?!
WE STRETCH OUR LEGS AND HAVE SOME LAUGHS!
WE BEGIN OUR MISSION, JOHNNY.

THIS WORLD NOW BELONGS TO THE CRIME SYNDICATE!

VARIANT COVER GALLERY

JUSTICE LEAGUE 18
Variant cover by Kenneth Rocafort & Blond

JUSTICE LEAGUE 19
Variant cover by Sergio Aragonés & Tom Luth

JUSTICE LEAGUE 19
Fold-out cover by Ivan Reis, Joe Prado & Rod Reis

JUSTICE LEAGUE 20
Variant cover by Tyler Kirkham, Sandra Hope Archer & Alex Sinclair

JUSTICE LEAGUE 23
Variant cover triptych by Mikel Janin, Vicente Cifuentes & Tomeu Morey

JUSTICE LEAGUE 22
Cover triptych by Ivan Reis, Joe Prado & Rod Reis

JUSTICE LEAGUE 22
Variant cover triptych by Brett Booth, Norm Rapmund & Andrew Dalhouse

JUSTICE LEAGUE 23
Cover triptych by Doug Mahnke & Alex Sinclair

BLOND

KIRKHAM

IVAN REIS
ROD REIS.

Booth "2013"
RAPMUND
House

JUSTICE LEAGUE #22
TRINITY WAR CHAPTER ONE

PAGE ONE.
PANEL ONE.

A WIDESCREEN PANEL ACROSS THE TOP OF THE PAGE

An establishing shot of "Chrystie Street" in Greenwich Village at night. It's raining hard. Few people are on the street - an old man with an umbrella walking his dog in the rain and now a YELLOW TAXI that's pulled up, from right to left, with its lights on - a nondescript white female with red hair, we'll call her BETH, in her 20s, is getting out of the cab, holding an open newspaper over her head as an umbrella. She ducks down and calls out to the driver.

1. CAPTION (XANADU): I haven't always done the right thing. In fact, I spent most of my life doing everything but.

2. BETH (DOUBLE BALLOON): You sure this is the place?

3. TAXI (DOUBLE BALLOON): You wanted Chrystie Street, didn't you?

4. BETH (DOUBLE BALLOON): Yes, but --

5. TAXI (DOUBLE BALLOON): This is the only Chrystie Street in Greenwich Village, hon.

6. CAPTION (XANADU): I believed myself wicked at heart and used my power in iniquitous ways.

PANEL TWO.
A longshot of Beth standing there alone in the rain as the cab drives off. Beth looks over at it, the red lights the only real lights on the street. Beth is still holding the newspaper over her head.

7. CAPTION (XANADU): I was lost.

8. BETH (DOUBLE BALLOON): WAIT!

9. BETH (DOUBLE BALLOON): It's not here!

10. CAPTION (XANADU): Then I met a magician named John Zatara. John taught me that it was never too late to choose a life of rectitude.

PANEL THREE.
CLOSE ON Beth, turning and looking up - seeing something she hadn't seen a second ago - as if it wasn't there. A soft light shines on her - as if it just turned on - the glow of NEON SIGNS.

PANEL FOUR.
The newspaper down at her side now, as if she were stunned, Beth stands very small in the foreground, her back to us - she's looking over to a storefront - in the window a neon sign reads: PSYCHIC READER - and another neon sign reads TAROT READINGS (under that) PAST, PRESENT and FUTURE. Another sign reads LIFE ADVISOR (Ivan, check out the reference we'll provide on MADAME XANADU'S PARLOR and update the storefront however you see fit - it should look mysterious and OPEN - beckoning this young woman to come inside.)

11. CAPTION (XANADU): He also taught me how to hide in plain sight.

12. BETH: Oh.

PANEL FIVE.
SMALL PANEL. VERY CLOSE ON Beth's hand opening the door to go inside - a bell on it rings.

13. CAPTION (XANADU): I sit in this shop waiting for those in distress to find their way to me.

PANEL SIX.
SMALL PANEL. VERY CLOSE ON the PAST, PRESENT and FUTURE neon sign.

14. CAPTION (XANADU): I see the tragedy in their futures.

PANEL SEVEN.
SMALL PANEL. The "FUTURE" word goes dark.

15. CAPTION (XANADU): And just as John did with me, I help them onto a different path.

SFX: kzzt

PANEL EIGHT.
CUT TO the interior of the shop. Beth walks in cautiously... there's all sorts of stereotypical psychic items there - Madame Xanadu hides in plain sight as an everyday "cheap" psychic, just like Zatanna hides as a stage magician.

16. CAPTION (XANADU): I sense this woman's desperation, though for some reason little else.

17. CAPTION (XANADU): But if I'm able I will help her.

18. BETH: H-hello?

19. BETH: Are you OPEN?

20. MADAME XANADU (O/P): I'm ALWAYS open.

CAFE
PSYCHIC READER
TAROT READINGS
PAST PRESENT FUTURE
ADVISOR
PAST
PRESENT
FUTURE
PAST
PRESENT
FUTURE

PAGE THREE.
PANEL ONE.

A WIDESCREEN PANEL ACROSS THE TOP OF THE PAGE

A VISION OF MANHATTAN BURNING AND CRUMBLED - the harbor filled with the DEAD. The sky is ON FIRE - AS RED AS THE WATER. There is no sign of the Statue of Liberty. Ivan, this should appear to be a vision of our world after a horrific attack...

In the FOREGROUND are silhouettes of SUPERMAN, WONDER WOMAN and BATMAN looking at the wreckage.

1. CAPTION (XANADU): But it's not HERS.

2. SUPERMAN-LIKE FIGURE: There's nothing left to fight for.

3. WONDER WOMAN-LIKE FIGURE: Yes, there is.

4. BATMAN-LIKE FIGURE: We have to escape. We have to save him.

5. CAPTION (XANADU): I see the AFTERMATH of a GREAT WAR. And I see one word that defines it: TRINITY.

PANEL TWO.
CUT BACK TO Beth and Madame Xanadu. Xanadu holds her head, a massive headache hits her. Beth is worried, scared.

6. BETH: What's WRONG with me?

7. CAPTION (XANADU): What is the TRINITY WAR?

8. MADAME XANADU: The CARDS.

PANEL THREE.
Madame Xanadu turns to one of her cards. There seems to be some kind of magical crackle as she turns the cards - a faint hint of electrical magic. SFX: kzzt

9. MADAME XANADU: The cards will tell me WHO will START it and HOW I can stop them.

PANEL FOUR.
CLOSE ON the first Tarot Card turned over -- it's of BILLY BATSON SHOUTING AND SHAZAM BEHIND HIM with a LIGHTNING BOLT icon in the background. But it doesn't say Shazam at the bottom, it just says - THE BOY.

Ivan, the cards should look like old-fashioned Tarot Cards - almost like flat woodprint versions of our characters when we see them.

SFX: fwap

10. CAPTION (XANADU): I have yet to meet him, but I know who he is.

11. CAPTION (XANADU): And how WRONGLY he was chosen.

DECTETIVE

PAGE TEN.

PANEL ONE.
CUT BACK TO Madame Xanadu, her hands putting down the BATMAN Tarot Card - labeled THE DETECTIVE.

SFX: fwap

PANEL TWO.
CUT TO the Watchtower - but it's lying battered on the coast of Rhode Island (where it was set down/crashed at the end of JUSTICE LEAGUE #20). It's on a rocky coast in the city of Happy Harbor, Rhode Island (which was the original location of the Justice League cave in their first BRAVE & THE BOLD appearances). It's night.

BATMAN and CYBORG are examining the wreckage. The satellite is HUGE, Ivan - as wide as a building, partially in the water. The waves crashing up against it.

1. BANNER: Happy Harbor, Rhode Island.

2. The remains of the Justice League Watchtower.

3. CYBORG: So someone hacks into our system WITHOUT my knowing, shuts down our defenses and lets DESPERO in.

4. CYBORG: While someone else -- or maybe the same person -- breaks into the Batcave and steals a Kryptonite ring.

5. CYBORG: A Kryptonite ring no one knew you had.

PANEL THREE.
CLOSER ON Cyborg and Batman. Cyborg looks over at Batman, who has a FLASHLIGHT in his hand as he looks through the wreckage.

6. BATMAN: I have it for STUDY, Vic.

7. CYBORG: To see if you can come up with a KRYPTONITE ANTIDOTE for Superman?

8. CYBORG: That might fly with the rookies, Bruce, but not with me.

PANEL FOUR.
We move to another area of the satellite - Element Woman has turned herself into a giant JACK to lift up a section of the Watchtower so Firestorm and the Atom can salvage what they can. Element Woman should look like Metamorpho when he changes - her face stretched over the white part - larger than life. There's a BIG SMILE on Element Woman's face. Firestorm is tossing debris over his shoulder - zapping it with a blast from one finger and turning it into gas. The Atom is small and going through debris.

9. ATOM: Batman said to keep our eyes out for anything salvageable from the trophy room, Element Woman.

10. FIRESTORM: I can't believe you stopped Despero all by yourself, Atom.

11. ELEMENT WOMAN: That is the COOLEST thing that's ever happened in the history of happenings.

12. ATOM: Yeah, uh, beginner's luck, I guess.

PANEL FIVE.
FLASHBACK to JUSTICE LEAGUE #20 - the Atom looks up at MARTIAN MANHUNTER who is hunched over DESPERO'S body in the wrecked Watchtower. The Atom gazes over at Manhunter, he gazes back to her.

13. MANHUNTER: Tell no one I was here.

PANEL SIX.
CLOSER ON the Atom, getting a little nervous that they might suspect something - she hides it by calling out as she moves through the wreckage.

14. ATOM: HEY! I think I found something!

PANEL SEVEN.
A WIDESCREEN PANEL ACROSS THE BOTTOM OF THE PAGE

She lifts up a piece of debris and finds a trophy - it's a CHESS SET from the League's original fight with DESPERO. The board is BLACK AND YELLOW CHECKERS. The pieces are lying on the ground - they should look like the oversimplified ones from JUSTICE LEAGUE OF AMERICA #1 (1960s). There's a chessboard and pieces: BATMAN, WONDER WOMAN, THE FLASH, AQUAMAN, GREEN LANTERN, CYBORG and MARTIAN MANHUNTER (in the New 52, this happened when he was on the team). The SUPERMAN piece is MISSING.

The Atom is small, so the pieces should be big - almost as big as her.

15. ATOM: It's a CHESS SET...

PAGE ELEVEN.

PANEL ONE.

CUT BACK TO Superman, Pandora and Diana. Superman walks up to Pandora with Diana, who has put her sword down – not sensing a threat any longer.

1. CAPTION (ATOM): "...but the SUPERMAN piece is MISSING."

2. SUPERMAN: Humans aren't evil because someone opened a MAGIC BOX, Pandora. Whoever told you that--

3. PANDORA: No one TOLD me ANYTHING. I was THERE. I SAW the SEVEN SINS fly out into the world.

4. SUPERMAN: I can't have this conversation. Diana?

5. WONDER WOMAN: That's what happened, Superman. My mother told me the story. Someone TRICKED her into opening the box.

PANEL TWO.

CLOSE ON Pandora, the hood shadowing her face.

6. PANDORA: But there's someone out there that can UNDO what I did. Someone that can OPEN this Box and IMPRISON sin once again.

7. PANDORA: We can FREE humanity from EVIL. And I can be free from my CURSE.

PANEL THREE.

Pandora shoves the Box into Superman's hands – Wonder Woman reaches out for him. Superman recoils in pain.

8. PANDORA: You just need to open the Box. And if ANYONE can SURVIVE its touch, it's SUPERMAN!

9. SUPERMAN (DOUBLE BALLOON): AHH!

PANEL FOUR.

VERY VERY CLOSE ON the FACE OF PANDORA'S BOX – THE THREE EYES.

10. WONDER WOMAN (O/P) (DOUBLE BALLOON): Superman?!

PAGE TWELVE.

SPLASH

A FULL FIGURE SHOT of SUPERMAN! Superman touches the Box – and arches back in pain, crying out. His suit goes BLACK. His skin goes PALE. A RED GLOWING SPOT ON THE CENTER OF HIS FOREHEAD – LIKE A THIRD EYE. His eyes glow RED. RED AND BLACK LIGHTNING EXPLODES FROM HIM.

1. SUPERMAN (DOUBLE BALLOON): AAHHHH!

CROP
BLEED

PAGE FIFTEEN.

PANEL ONE.
CUT TO the Atom, very small - hidden among the debris of the Justice League
Watchtower. She speaks, a finger at her ear as she activates her JLA com in her mask. There is a little INSET panel of ELEMENT WOMAN that points to her. (These inset panels are described in greater detail in panel six on this page.)

1. CAPTION (BATMAN): "We're already making a call."

2. ATOM: YES! We're heading into Kahndaq right now, Colonel Trevor.

3. ATOM: What do I do?

PANEL TWO.
CUT BACK TO a sad Doctor Light in his office, his helmet still off and on his desk. He sits in the dark, his head hung low - hands holding it up. He has no one to talk to anymore - he doesn't dare risk contacting his wife about this again.

4. WALLER (ELECTRIC - DISEMBODIED): Doctor Light.

PANEL THREE.
Doctor Light looks over at a JLA COMMUNICATOR (like an iPhone) sitting on his desk by the Firestorm, Ronnie and Jason pictures - beyond it his family photo.

5. WALLER/JLA COMMUNICATOR (ELECTRIC): Get your helmet strapped on and get to the Jet.

PANEL FOUR.
CUT TO the hangar where the Justice League of America keep their INVISIBLE JET, which is a huge military plane that can "cloak" itself invisible.

MARTIAN MANHUNTER leads the Justice League of America to the plane - HAWKMAN, KATANA, CATWOMAN, STARGIRL, VIBE and GREEN LANTERN/SIMON BAZ.

There are A.R.G.U.S. Agents working on the plane.

6. CAPTION (WALLER): "The Justice League is heading into Kahndaq.

7. CAPTION (WALLER): "Your job is to get them OUT by ANY means possible."

8. CAPTION: The JLA's Invisible Jet.

PANEL FIVE.
CUT TO Steve and Waller in Waller's office. Steve is geared up, files of the JUSTICE LEAGUE - including the headshots - in his hands. He's going to pass them to the various members.

9. STEVE: They aren't READY for this, Waller.

10. WALLER: This is an OPPORTUNITY we might not get again, Steve.

11. WALLER: This our chance to go shine a SPOTLIGHT on how UNCONTROLLABLE the Justice League is -

PANEL SIX.
Moving across Vibe who takes a seat with the other Leaguers, sitting next to Stargirl. Vibe is flipping through the Flash file. (Ivan, I'm thinking maybe each member - as we cycle through - has a little square inset panel by them with a line to them - in this panel Vibe would have a little square inset panel of THE FLASH while Stargirl would have a little square inset panel of CYBORG - these would be the same HEADSHOT panels as seen in pages 8/9. Only the JUSTICE LEAGUE have inset square panels, the JLA are in panel.)

12. CAPTION (WALLER): "—and how the JLA is the only team the world can TRUST."

13. VIBE: This is like defcon NEGATIVE ELEVEN, Stargirl.

14. VIBE: Colonel Trevor handed me a FOLDER on THE FLASH and said he was my TARGET. This is CRAZY.

15. STARGIRL: What can I do against Cyborg?

PANEL SEVEN.
Vibe looks over at Hawkman, who is reading Aquaman's file. (And like the above, there's a little inset square panel of AQUAMAN with a line to Hawkman.)

16. VIBE: You got AQUAMAN? You don't, uh, you don't want to TRADE, do you, Hawkman?

17. HAWKMAN: NO.

18. HAWKMAN: But I'll take yours too if you don't think you can handle it.

PANEL EIGHT.
Catwoman is flipping through Batman's file - which to her is incomplete. Katana sitting next to her. (And like the above, we have a little square inset panel of BATMAN with a line to Catwoman and a little square inset panel of WONDER WOMAN with Katana.)

In the back, Vibe notices that the LIGHTS are getting dim.

19. CATWOMAN: Whatever they're doing, if Batman's involved, we should trust them.

20. KATANA: Your personal investment is clouding your judgment, Catwoman.

21. CATWOMAN: Hey, worry about your own target, Katana.

22. CATWOMAN (SMALL): As if that matchup makes ANY sense.

23. VIBE: Hey, why's it getting DARK in here?

24. DOCTOR LIGHT (O/P): This is WRONG.

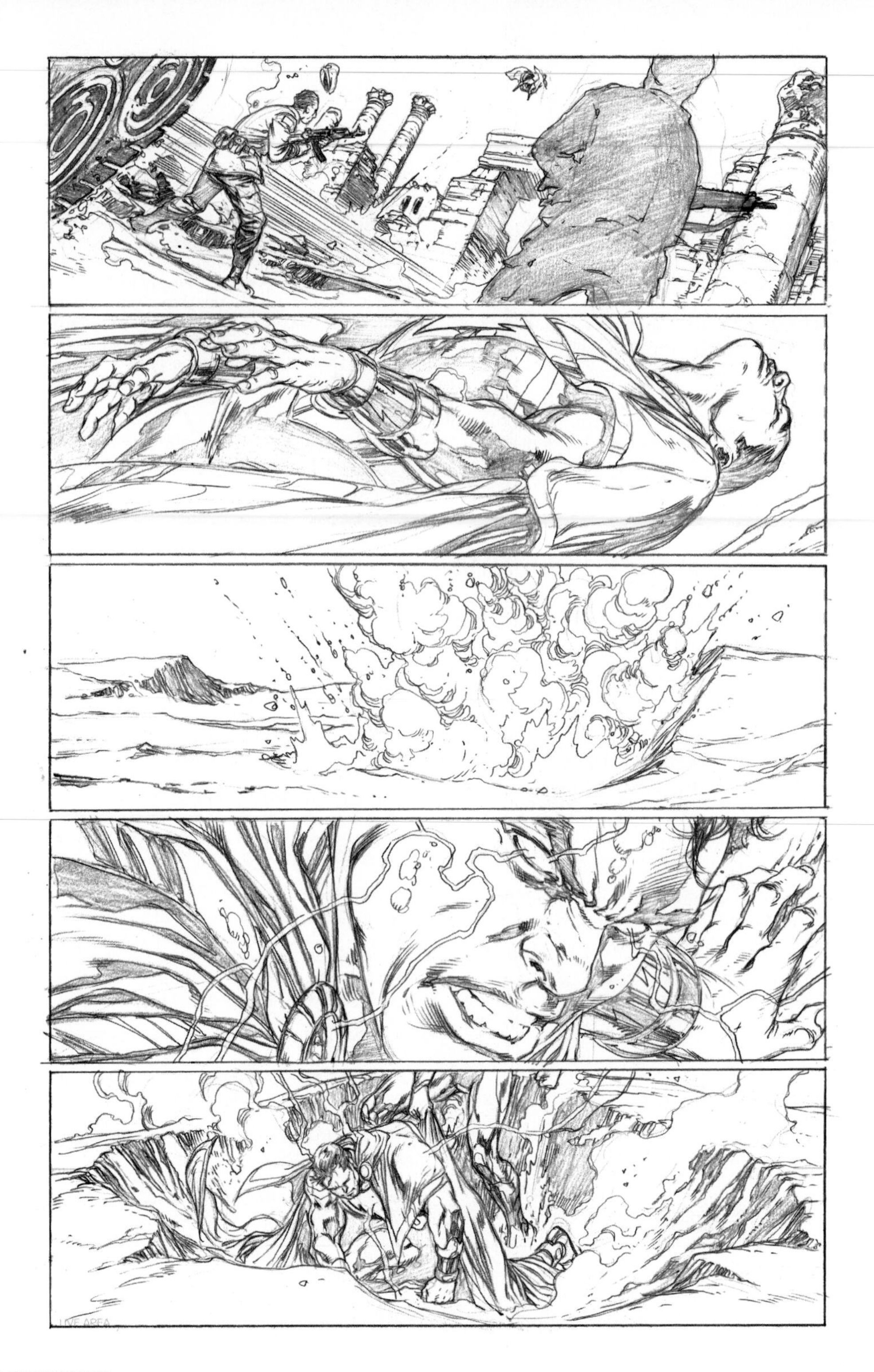

PAGE EIGHTEEN.

PANEL ONE.

But before Shazam can throw his punch he's hit by something INCREDIBLY STRONG – a BLUR of RED, BLUE and a tiny bit of YELLOW – Superman, of course – hits him from left to right. Shazam goes flying. [NO DIALOGUE.]

PANEL TWO.

An extreme longshot of Shazam flying through the air – into the desert.

[NO DIALOGUE.]

PANEL THREE.

Shazam lands like a BOMB in the desert. He hits a dune – sending most of it up into the air.

[NO DIALOGUE.]

PANEL FOUR.

CLOSE ON Shazam gazing up, electricity in his eyes. He's not happy...

1. SHAZAM: Who's asking for a FIGHT?

PANEL FIVE.

Suddenly, something tugs on Shazam's cape.

2. SUPERMAN (O/P): No one wants one.

PAGE NINTEEN.
PANEL ONE.

LARGE PANEL
Shazam turns around and swings hard – SLAMMING his fist right into Superman, who is taken aback – and hurt by the MAGIC of it all. Electricity explodes all around!

1. SHAZAM: Then you shouldn't have STARTED it!

PANEL TWO.
Superman slides across the desert – like the space shuttle landing – kicking up sand.

[NO DIALOGUE.]

PANEL THREE.
CLOSE ON Shazam, realizing he just knocked down Superman – UH OH.

2. SHAZAM: SUPERMAN?

3. SHAZAM: I just knocked down Superman.

PANEL FOUR.
SAME EXACT PANEL AS ABOVE, but Shazam realizes HE JUST KNOCKED DOWN SUPERMAN! He smiles.

4. SHAZAM: I JUST KNOCKED DOWN SUPERMAN.

PANEL FIVE.
A WIDESCREEN PANEL ACROSS THE BOTTOM OF THE PAGE

A LONGSHOT of Superman flying from right to left and slamming into Shazam! There's an explosion of lightning! Wind kicks up the sand!

WHO IS THE EVIL
BEHIND THE EVIL
EVIL
EVIL
DARKSEID'S INVADES
SUPER VILLAINS
HAVE A NICE EVIL DAY
STRANGE LIGHTS ABOVE THE KIELDER FOREST

PAGE TWENTY-SIX.

SPLASH

We're standing behind The Question and gazing up at his crazy conspiracy theory board – but it's the entire wall of the warehouse!!! He should be very small, a full figure shot. The wall is full of images and words tied together by strings.

Words from various newspaper articles form a large question on the top of the board:

WHO IS THE EVIL BEHIND THE EVIL?

All the strings point from various Post-Its and photographs of crime scenes, missing persons cases, etc. Some specifics are: an image of Pandora from the bleachers in JUSTICE LEAGUE #1, an image of THE PHANTOM STRANGER as seen battling THE SPECTRE in recent Phantom Stranger issues, an image of SUPERMAN and WONDER WOMAN kissing as seen in JUSTICE LEAGUE OF AMERICA #1, an image of AMANDA WALLER, an image of the screen from the end of JUSTICE LEAGUE #18 with the skull & crossbones and HAVE A NICE DAY written across it, a newspaper article that reads: STRANGE LIGHTS ABOVE THE KIELDER FOREST, a word made up of different letters from various magazines and newspapers – S-U-P-E-R- V-I-L-L-A-I-N-S, a newspaper article that reads: DARKSEID INVADES with an image of the JUSTICE LEAGUE fighting Parademons – AND FINALLY, THERE'S AN IMAGE OF SUPERMAN IN THE VERY CENTER OF THE COLLAGE – ALL THE STRINGS ARE POINTING TOWARD HIM.

1. THE QUESTION: WHO IS THE EVIL BEHIND THE EVIL?

PAGES THIRTY AND THIRTY-ONE.

PANEL ONE.
BIG PANEL ACROSS THE TOP OF THE PAGE

The storefront of Madame Xanadu EXPLODES with ORANGE FIRE – the windows and door incinerated as the powerful flames and force shoot out of the storefront. A passerby is blown backwards.

[NO DIALOGUE.]

PANEL TWO.
CLOSE ON the Atom on the ground, pleading with everyone – fearful and almost in tears. But she's SO SMALL compared to the FEET STOMPING AROUND.

She's almost stepped on by HAWKMAN'S BOOT!

1. ATOM (DOUBLE BALLOON): STOP!

PANEL THREE.
BACK TO the aftermath of the explosion – flames dancing among the debris. The shop and a car outside still burning. Charred tarot cards fluttering down like leaves from a tree – some of them on fire.

[NO DIALOGUE.]

PANEL FOUR.
Back to panel two's fight, but we PULL BACK FURTHER from the Atom and see PARTS of our heroes fighting. Part of KATANA – Part of WONDER WOMAN. She continues to cry out – her voice being less and less heard.

2. ATOM (SMALLER): Please stop!

PANEL FIVE.
BACK TO the aftermath of the explosion – three cards float down from above – THE TRINITY OF SIN! PANDORA – THE PAWN. THE QUESTION – THE UNKNOWN. And now THE PHANTOM STRANGER – labeled simply THE BETRAYER.

[NO DIALOGUE.]

PANEL SIX.
And now the Atom is extremely small – her voice drowned out by the violence – we barely even see her. We now see MARTIAN MANHUNTER move past her. Again, it's a BLUR of BATTLE.

3. ATOM (EVEN SMALLER): Please!

PAGES THIRTY-TWO AND THIRTY-THREE.

PANEL ONE.

A VERY VERY THIN PANEL ACROSS THE TOP TWO PAGES

STRAIGHT DOWN ON SEVERAL OF THE OTHER TAROT CARDS SCATTERED IN THE STREET IN FRONT OF MADAME XANADU'S. Like the others, the pictures are labeled with not their name but a simple descriptor.

CYBORG – THE GRID.
FIRESTORM – THE PRISONER. (though the ER in PRISONER is partly burned/ripped)
THE ATOM – THE GAMEPLAYER.
ELEMENT WOMAN – THE FREAK.
THE FLASH – THE MESSENGER.
AQUAMAN – THE KING.
ZATANNA – THE MAGICIAN.

PANEL TWO.

A DOUBLE-PAGE SPREAD

MOST OF THE TWO PAGES!!!

CUT BACK TO the JUSTICE LEAGUE vs. THE JUSTICE LEAGUE OF AMERICA – it's back on! And in the biggest way – in the main image here of the spread is SUPERMAN vs. MARTIAN MANHUNTER!

The other heroes start attacking their respective members – VIBE blasts THE FLASH – but misses, STARGIRL hits CYBORG, CATWOMAN leaps on BATMAN. [NO DIALOGUE.]

PANEL THREE.
JUST LIKE PANEL ONE – A VERY VERY THIN PANEL ACROSS THE BOTTOM.

STRAGHT DOWN ON SEVERAL OTHER TAROT CARDS SCATTERED IN THE STREET IN NEW YORK.

GREEN ARROW – THE ARCHER.
CATWOMAN – THE THIEF.
STARGIRL – THE SPIRIT.
SIMON BAZ/GREEN LANTERN – THE MIRACLE WORKER.
VIBE – THE MISFIT.
HAWKMAN – THE SAVAGE.
KATANA – THE ASSASSIN.

THE DECTETIVE
THE SACRIFICE
THE HERO
THE WARRIOR
THE OUTSIDER
CREDITS
LIVE AREA

PAGE THIRTY-FOUR.

PANEL ONE.

MOST OF THE PAGE

We're on the street outside of Madame Xanadu's shop - looking straight down at the burning debris and among them THREE TAROT CARDS. In the lower center is the card with DOCTOR LIGHT, which is now burned and charred, representing his death. We can read his descriptor underneath it: THE SACRIFICE.

Arching around it are three more cards. To the right of the Doctor Light card is - BATMAN - though it reads THE DETECTIVE - then above the Doctor Light card - SUPERMAN - though it reads THE HERO (though "HERO" has a BLACK SLASH through it) - and then to the right of the Doctor Light card - WONDER WOMAN - though it reads THE WARRIOR.

There are hints of the other cards of each character around them that we've seen throughout the issue.

1. CAPTION (NEWS): "...reports coming in now of an all-out WAR between the
JUSTICE LEAGUE and the JUSTICE LEAGUE OF AMERICA.

2. CAPTION (NEWS): "...ONE CASUALTY already...I'm not sure I believe it...at the hands of SUPERMAN?

PANEL TWO.
CUT TO the Leader of the Secret Society sitting in his chair in his office as established in JUSTICE LEAGUE OF AMERICA #2. He watches a televised report of the battle between the Justice Leagues.

3. NEWS (ELECTRIC): This can't be true.

4. LEADER: Ha.

PANEL THREE.
CLOSE ON the Leader's mouth and chin - a slight smile on his pale skin. WHO IS HE?

5. LEADER: Thanks to ME, everyone will actually BELIEVE that Superman's KILLED Doctor Light.

PANEL FOUR.
And we finally end CLOSE on one of the cards - the silhouette of THE LEADER of the Secret Society with the hat and cane - and his descriptor reads: THE OUTSIDER. There are THREE STARS around the image in the sky - signifying another trinity.

6. CAPTION (LEADER): "And by the time the Justice League figures out what I'm up to, the WORLD will already belong to US."

A BLACK BAR FOR THE CREDITS ALONG THE BOTTOM

TITLE: TRINITY WAR: CHAPTER ONE TITLE:
THE DEATH CARD
WRITER: Geoff Johns
PENCILS: Ivan Reis
INKS: Joe Prado
COLORS: Rod Reis
LETTERS: DC Lettering
ASSISTANT EDITOR: Kate Stewart
SENIOR EDITOR: Brian Cunningham

DC COMICS™

"Welcoming to new fans looking to get into superhero comics for the first time and old fans who gave up on the funny-books long ago."
—SCRIPPS HOWARD NEWS SERVICE

START AT THE BEGINNING!

JUSTICE LEAGUE VOLUME 1: ORIGIN

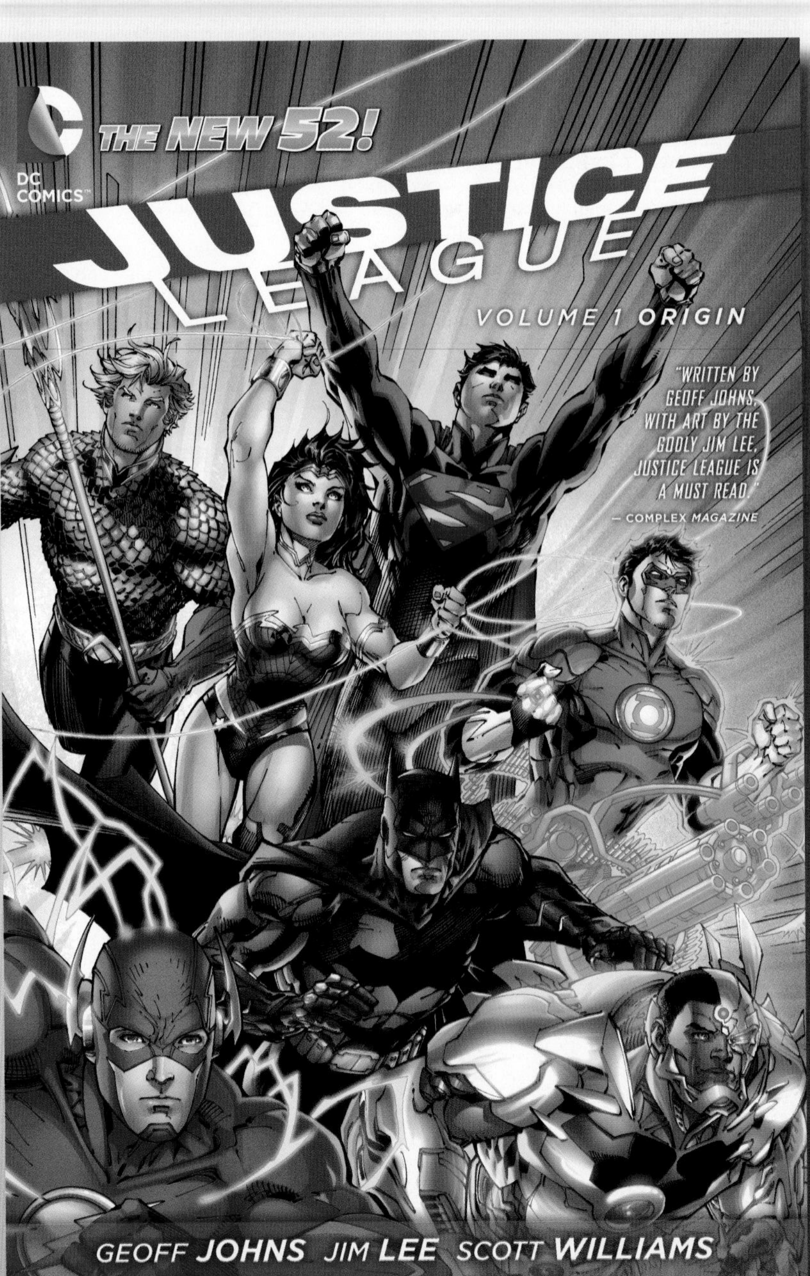

AQUAMAN VOLUME 1: THE TRENCH

THE SAVAGE HAWKMAN VOLUME 1: DARKNESS RISING

GREEN ARROW VOLUME 1: THE MIDAS TOUCH

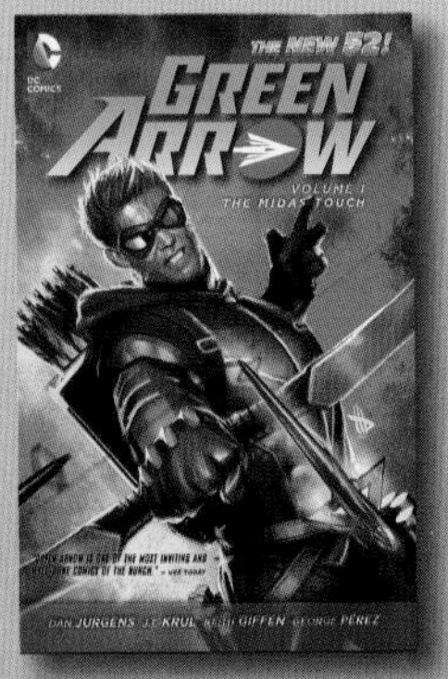

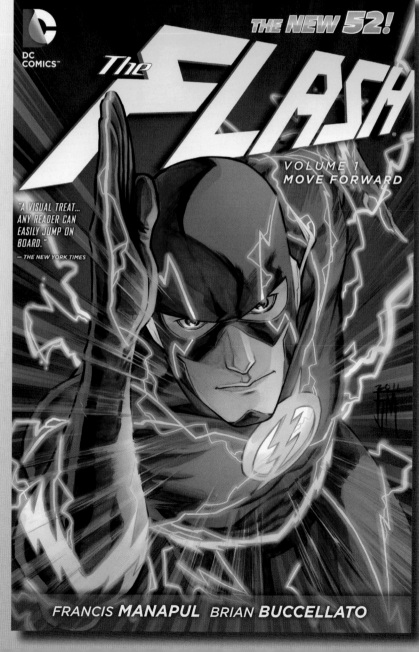

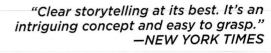

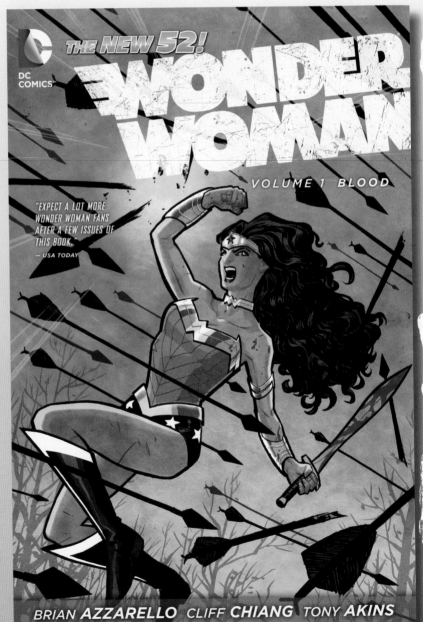